WASHINGTON COUNTY ARKANSAS

Sheriff's Census
for
1865

Nancy Maxwell

HERITAGE BOOKS
2008

HERITAGE BOOKS
AN IMPRINT OF HERITAGE BOOKS, INC.

Books, CDs, and more—Worldwide

For our listing of thousands of titles see our website
at
www.HeritageBooks.com

Published 2008 by
HERITAGE BOOKS, INC.
Publishing Division
100 Railroad Ave. #104
Westminster, Maryland 21157

International Standard Book Numbers
Paperbound: 978-1-55613-885-0
Clothbound: 978-0-7884-7521-4

PREFACE

Article IV, Section 30 of the 1864 Arkansas state constitution includes the following directive:

> "An enumeration of the inhabitants of the state shall be taken under the direction of the general assembly on the first day of January, one thousand eight hundred and sixty-five, and at the end of every ten years thereafter..."

The 1865 sheriff's census of Washington County, Arkansas is the only county census known to exist from this enumeration. Its importance lies in its having been taken just nine months after the end of the Civil War when the county was still recovering from major loss of life and property. Homes, schools, and businesses had been severely damaged or destroyed, livestock and crops were destroyed or taken by Union and Confederate forces, and bushwhackers roamed the countryside. The high rate of loss is evident from the 442 claims for personal property reimbursement filed with Southern Claims Commission after the war, more than double the number of the county with the second-largest number of claims. See Gary B. Mills, Civil War Claims in the South: An Index of Civil War Damage Claims Filed Before the Southern Claims Commission, 1871-1880, Laguna Hills, CA: Aegean Park Press, 1980.

The war also took its toll on the population. According to the typescript title page of the 1865 census, 5,887 persons had been enumerated. If this is count is anywhere near accurate, the total county population was down by about 9,000 from the 1860 census, which put the total population at 14,640. Given the condition of the county immediately after the war, there is probably some discrepancy in the actual numbers. Growth resumed after the war and by 1870 the recorded population was 17,264.

It is hoped that researchers with roots in northwest Arkansas will be able to identify their ancestors who first appeared or who had remained in Washington County during the watershed years of 1861-1865.

The original census was microfilmed by David W. Bizzell, who was appointed Pulaski County historian in 1955, and was that county's deputy county clerk from 1957-1975. Gratitude is expressed to Mr. Russell P. Baker, Deputy Director of the Arkansas History Commission in Little Rock, who gave permission for a microfilm copy of this census to be purchased and abstracted. The Commission owns a microfilm copy of the census which is available for public use. According to the title page preceeding the census, the original manuscript is in the AHC manuscript collection.

According to the title page of this census, 5,887 persons were enumerated in Washington County, Arkansas on 15 December 1865. The first identified township is Clear Creek, and does not appear in the heading until page 13 of the original census. It is not known whether the persons on pages 1 to 13 were enumerated in Clear Creek or were in another township. The named townships in order of appearance are Clear Creek, Elm Spring, Marrs Hill, Illinois, Vineyard, Cove Creek, Mountain, West Fork, White River, Richland, Prairie, and the city of Fayetteville. Cane Hill and Brush Creek Townships are not named, even though they existed at the time the census was taken. Townships and their enumeration dates sometimes begin in the middle of a column of names. Townships appear in this abstract but the dates have been omitted. The census is arranged chronologically with the earliest date being 2 March 1866 in Clear Creek Township.

ARRANGEMENT

The left page on the microfilm copy of the original census contains the names and age groups. The right page contains headings for free persons of color by gender, and headers of an agricultural nature. Headers on most pages include the following personal information:

White males under 10 years
White males over 10 and under 18 years
White males over 18 and under 21 years
White males over 21 and under 45 years
White males over 45 years
White females under 16 years
White females over 16 years
Free persons of color - male and female

Acres of land cultivated for cotton
Acres of land cultivated for grain
Bales of cotton
Bushels of corn
Bushels of wheat
Bushels of oats

Headers appear on most of the original census, but toward the end some headers are only partially given, or as can be seen on pages 312-347, do not appear at all.

This book includes only the name, sex, and age of each white person and does not include the agricultural information.

PAGINATION

Pagination of the original census in inconsistent and confusing in the first few pages and in the pages following page 307. Neither side of the first page is numbered. Both sides of the second page were given the number 2, and the third page is 7. After page 7, the left-side pages are odd-numbered and the right-side pages are even-numbered. The left-side-odd-right-side-even pattern of page numbering is consistent from page 7 to page 307, when the next left-side page is numbered 308. Even-numbering of left-side pages continues to page 322. There is no page 323 or 324. Page 325 immediately follows page 322. There is no page 326 or 327; page 328 immediately follows page 325. Numbering is even on left-side pages from page 328 to page 342. There is no page 343; page 345 immediately follows page 342, and the odd-numbering of left-side pages continues from page 345 to page 353. There is no page 355; page 356 immediately follows page 353. Left-side pages are even-numbered from page 356 to page 390. Page 393 immediately follows page 390 and continues the odd-numbering pattern to page 405.

In this book, the original pagination appears in brackets in the upper left-hand side of each new section of names. Pagination in the index refers to the number at the bottom of the page in this book. Researchers should use the bracketed page numbers to find names in the original census.

On using the microfilm, researchers will find the following original census pages duplicated in the microfilming process: 151, 181, 251, 267, 299, 324, and 388.

SPELLING

Many names were very difficult to read or were badly misspelled. All names were copied as they appeared in the record or were deciphered using best judgement. Other sources should be used to determine correct spelling.

HOUSEHOLDS

A few dividing lines distinguishing one household from another can be found on various pages throughout the census. This method of separation appears to have been the exception rather than the rule and has not been included in this book. Persons within a household generally appear to be listed by head of household, with children generally listed from oldest to youngest regardless of sex. Age and sex of some persons were not marked by the enumerator and so are indicated here by the words 'No entry' in the age and sex columns. Ages of persons of either sex that were marked in an opposite-sex column were copied as they appeared and are identified in this book by an asterisk. Free persons of color were identified only by name and sex and are found in this book by the letters "FPC" in the age column.

MISCELLANEOUS INFORMATION CONCERNING THE ORIGINAL CENSUS

On pages 50, 52, 53, and 54, ages of white females were marked in white-male columns, possibly giving the researcher narrower age ranges. Other sources should be used to verify or disprove them.

On pages 334, 338, and 345, too many columns made age identifications difficult. Best judgement was used to place ages in correct columns. Other sources should be used to determine their accuracy.

On page 351, there is no "Over 45" column under the "White Males" header.

An "Over 16 and under 45" column appears under the "White Females" header but no marks appear in that column.

On pages 370, 384, and 386, an "Over 45" column is under the "White Females" header.

On page 403, only the first three age columns appear under the "White Males" header.

TABLE OF CONTENTS

Page numbers are listed for the original census and for this book to make it easy to find a given township and date if available.

[1]		
HAMMOND Eveline	f	16+
HAMMOND Emeline	f	16+
ANTONEY Elihu	m	21-45
ANTONEY Mary	f	16+
ANTONEY William	m	0-10
SHARP Manerva	f	16+
SHARP James	m	10-18
SHARP William	m	10-18
SHARP Mary	No entry	
SHARP Thomas	m	10-18
SHARP G W	m	10-18
SHARP Francis M	m	0-10
ENYART John	m	45+
ENYART Nancy A	f	16+
ENYART Narsisy	f	16+
ENYART Annaliza	f	16+
ENYART John M	m	10-18
ENYART Steaphen B	m	10-18
ENYART Sarah L	f	0-16
ENYART Ebeneser	m	0-10
BUCKLEY J S	m	45+
BUCKLEY Nancy	f	16+
BUCKLEY Margret A	f	16+
BUCKLEY G W	m	18-21
BUCKLEY [torn] E	f	0-16

[2]		
BUCKLEY Benjamin F	m	10-18
BUCKLEY James H	m	10-18
BUCKLEY William L	m	0-10
BUCKLEY Ellive J	m	0-10
GAROTT C F	m	45+
GAROTT Susan	f	16+
GARROTT Sarah	f	16+
GARROTT Sarah E	f	0-16
GARROTT Charity	f	0-16
GARROTT Elizabeth	f	0-16
GARROTT James	m	0-10
MAYFIELD Matilda	f	16+
MAYFIELD Marthy	f	0-16
HICKSON Harrit	f	0-16
MAYFIELD Polley	f	0-16
MAYFIELD Ellender	f	0-16
MAYFIELD Lucinda	f	0-16
MAYFIELD Arramanda	f	0-16
MAYFIELD Wilbern G	m	0-10
SMITH James F	No entry	
SMITH Belzora	m	0-10
MAYFIELD Eliza	f	16+
MAYFIELD Sarah J	f	0-16
MAYFIELD Louisa	No entry	
MAYFIELD William	m	0-10

[7]		
MAYFIELD John	m	0-10
LANGLEY J K	m	45+
LANGLEY Susan	f	16+
OBRINE Sarah	f	16+
OBRINE Mary	f	16+
OBRINE Laticia J	f	16+
OBRINE William M	m	10-18
OBRINE Margret M	f	0-16
OBRINE John A	m	0-10
CLURE Luis W	m	45+
CLOURE Sarah	f	16+
CLURE J B	m	21-45
CLOUR Corley Elizabeth	f	16+
JOSICE Elexander	m	45+
JOICE Surrenia	f	16+
JOICE Malicia	f	16+
JOICE John Elexander	m	10-18
JOICE Margaret	f	0-16
JOICE Adalin	f	0-16
JOICE Theo Dosai	f	0-16
ALISON Aloxander	m	45+
ALISON Sarah	f	16+
ALISON Robert	m	21-45
ALISON Wm	m	21-45
ALISON Jame	m	21-45
ALISON L D	m	21-45
ALISON Jas	m	21-45
ALISON Elizabeath	f	0-16
ALISON John	m	18-21

[9]		
CLATON Willis	m	21-45
CLAYTON Mary	f	0-16
CLAYTON Margaret	f	16+
CLAYTON Joseph	m	10-18
CLAYTON Sarah	f	0-16
CLAYTON Noa	m	10-18
CAYTON William	m	0-10
CLAYTON John	m	0-10
CLAYTON Manerva	f	0-16
CLAYTON Mary	f	0-16
DUTON J H	m	21-45
DUTON Margret	f	16+
DUTON Thomas	m	0-10
DUTON Henry	m	0-10
DUTTON Gorge	m	0-10
DUTTON Moses	m	45+
DUTTON Elizbath	f	16+
DUTTON Mathy	f	16+
DUTTON Magaret	f	0-16
DUTTON James	m	10-18
DUTTON Nancy	f	0-16

DUTTON J Dillia	f	0-16	EATASIS Myley A	f	16+
DUTTON Chelysea	f	0-16	RISLEY John W	m	10-18
DUTTON Moses	m	0-10	ROBBERTS James J	m	45+
CLAYTON F	m	21-45	ROBBERTS Sinthey	f	16+
CLAYTON Nancy Weniford	f	16+	ROBBERTS Thomas M	m	21-45
CLAYTON Margret Sarfiony	f	0-16	ROBBERTS L E	f	16+
CLAYTON Thomas Stanford	m	10-18	ROBBERTS Nancy	f	16+
			ROBBERTS Margret A	f	0-16
			ROBBERTS Jane M	f	0-16
[11]			ROBBERTS Sinthy	f	0-16
CURK James Julis	m	18-21	ROBBERTS James J	m	10-18
CURK Sousan	f	16+	ROBBERTS Hulcea	f	0-16
JOHNSON Andrew	m	45+	ROBBERTS William A	m	0-10
JOHNSON Rachal	f	16+	ROBBERTS Lucy R	f	0-16
CLOORE Mary E	f	16+			
CLOER Johnithan	m	10-18			
CLOER Sarah A	f	0-16	[15]		
CLORE Marthey	f	0-16	SMILEY Hugh	m	21-45
CLORE Angeline	f	0-16	SMILEY E C	f	16+
CLORRE Georg W	m	0-10	SMILEY John	m	10-18
FINLEY Harriet	f	16+	SMILEY Amanda J	f	0-16
FINLEY Nancy E	f	16+	SMILEY Susan C	f	0-16
FINLEY William G	m	10-18	SMILEY William M	m	0-10
FINLEY Rebeca T	f	0-16	REED John	m	45+
FINLEY Alice J	f	0-16	REED Sarah	f	16+
FINLEY Samuel E	m	0-10	REED Nancy M	f	16+
ATWOOD Evans	m	18-21	REED Margret A	f	0-16
GRAHAM Ketorah	f	16+	REED Lewis J	m	0-10
GRAHAM Liza	f	16+	REED Albert M	m	0-10
GRAHAM Mary	f	16+	REED Levy B	m	0-10
GRAHAM Jessie	m	0-16	REED Robt B	m	0-10
GRAHAM Margret	f	0-16	SHERROD Wm H	m	45+
GRAHAM James W	m	0-10	SHERROD Elennor	f	16+
GRAHAM Silus	m	0-10	HUNTER Marthey	f	16+
GRAHAM Annie	f	0-16	SHERROD Sarah C	f	16+
SIMES Henry	m	45+	SHERROD Nancy E	f	16+
SIMES Elizabeath A	f	16+	SHERROD Leucina J	f	16+
SIMES William H	m	0-10	HUNTER John P	m	10-18
			SHERROD Arther J	m	10-18
			SHERROD Samui W	m	10-18
[13]			SHERROD Marthey A	f	0-16
CLEAR CREEK TOWNSHIP			SHERROD Susan	f	0-16
GRAHAM Moses	m	21-45	SHERROD William H	m	0-10
GRAHAM Debby Jane	f	16+	STAFORD Margret	f	16+
GRAHAM Lithey J	f	0-16	STAFFORD Evan	m	18-21
GRAHAM Polly	f	0-16	STAFFORD Andrew J	m	10-18
GRAHAM Rebeca	No entry		STAFORD Gorge W	m	10-18
GRAHAM James W	m	0-10			
GRAHAM Malayar	f	0-16			
GRAHAM Ben W	m	0-10	[17]		
GRAHAM Decia	f	0-16	LINLEY J Hugo	m	45+
LOYONS W E	m	21-45	LINLEY Dosia	f	16+
LYONS Feby	f	16+	Eliza	f	0-16
LYONS James R	m	0-10	John	m	21-45
LYONS William J	m	0-10	WHITE D A	m	FPC

Name	Sex	Age
WHITE Rosanar	f	16+
WHITE W C	m	21-45
DAGGOT L J	f	16+
DAGGOT P H	m	45+
VERNON Lucinda	f	16+
VERNON Nancy	f	0-16
VERNON James	m	0-10
VERNON Marthey	f	0-16
VERNON John	m	0-10
VERNON Sarah	f	0-16
LICKLITER Rufus	m	18-21
WILSON Rebeca	f	16+
WILSON Susan	f	16+
WILSON Hosaa	m	18-21
WILSON Elizabeath	f	16+
WILSON Morton	m	18-21
WILSON Benjamin	m	18-21
WILSON Lenpa	f	16+
WILSON Sanford	m	10-18
WILSON Harriet	f	16+
WILSON Wesley	m	0-10

[19]

Name	Sex	Age
WHITE Hulda	f	16+
WHITE Manerva	f	16+
WHITE Sally	f	16+
WHITE Emiline	f	16+
WHITE Burges	m	18-21
WHITE Burton	m	18-21
WHITE William	m	18-21
WHITE Shessley	m	10-18
WHITE Feba		No entry
WHITE Telitha	f	0-16
WHITE Nancy		No entry
WHITE Leucinda	f	0-16
WHITE Nicolous		No entry
ATWOOD Simon	m	45+
ATWOOD Eliza	f	16+
ATWOOD William M	m	18-21
HUET Alison	m	18-21
HUET Eley	f	16+
HUET George	m	10-18
HUET Alice	f	0-16
HUET Dan	m	0-10
HUET William	m	0-10
HUET John	m	0-10
HUET Hugh	m	0-10
PHILLIPPS Wilson	m	21-45
PHILLIPPS Artemicia	f	16+
PHILLIPPS Thomas F	m	10-18
PHILLIPPS Robt S	m	10-18

Name	Sex	Age
PHILLIPPS Lewis H	m	0-10

[21]

Name	Sex	Age
PHILLIPPS Betsey	f	0-16
PHILLIPPS Marthey A	f	0-16
PHILLIPPS Andrew	m	0-10
FITZGEARLDS Lucinda	f	16+
FITZGEARLDS Annie	f	16+
FITZGEARLDS William H	m	10-18
FITZGEARLDS Marion	f	0-16
FITZGEARLDS Benjamin	m	0-10
SNEAD B H	m	21-45
SNEAD Sinthey J	f	16+
GRAHAM James S	m	21-45
GRAHAM Rebeca J	f	16+
GRAHAM Rachal	f	16+
GRAHAM Dourthey	f	0-16
GRAHAM Benjamin	m	10-18
GRAHAM Amanda J	f	0-16
GRAHAM Orlena J	f	0-16
GRAHAM William P	m	0-10
GOODMAN Jessie	m	45+
GOODMAN Annie	f	16+
GOODMAN Perry	m	10-18
GOODMAN Liza J	f	0-16
GOODMAN Rufus	m	0-10
GOODMAN John	m	0-10
GOODMAN Jerome	m	0-10
GOODMAN Alfred	m	0-10
GOODMAN Charles E	m	0-10

[23]

Name	Sex	Age
HARTLEY H G	m	21-45
HARTLEY Theorlus	f	0-16
HARTLEY Rufus	m	10-18
HARTLEY Cornealey	f	0-16
HARTLEY Margret	f	0-16
HARTLEY John	m	21-45
HARTLEY Martin L	m	0-10
SEARCY A H	m	21-45
SEARCEY Leander	m	10-18
SEARCY Wesley	m	10-18
SEARCY Maranda	f	0-16
SEARCY Harriet	f	0-16
SEARCY William	m	0-10
GRAHAM Elizabeath	f	16+
GRAHAM Acey	m	0-10
GRAHAM Peter	m	0-10
GRAHAM Rebeca	f	0-16
GRAHAM Penelope	f	16+
GRAHAM Charles	m	0-10

LICKLITER John H	m	21-45
LICKLITER Louisa A	f	16+
LICKLITER Margret H	f	16+
LICKLITER Mary J	f	16+
LICKLITER William M	m	10-18
LICKLITER George A	m	10-18
LICKLITER Richard M	m	0-10

[25]

STONE Leroy D	m	21-45
STONE Nancy	f	16+
DALEY Susan	f	16+
STONE Luelsey	f	16+
STONE Luesey	f	16+
STONE John	m	10-18
STONE Willice	m	10-18
STONE Henry	m	0-10
STONE Albert	m	0-10
STONE Cidney	m	0-10
STONE Francis D	m	0-10
BLUDSAN Wm	m	21-45
BLUDSAN Sarah	f	16+
EXENDINE Marthey	f	16+
ANDERSON Andrew	m	10-18
ANDERSON Mary	m*	10-18
BLUDSAN John	m	0-10
BLEDSAN William L	m	0-10
McGARRAH Math	m	45+
McGARRAH Marthey	f	16+
McGARAH Malinda	f	16+
McGARRAH Nancy	f	16+
McGARRAH Wm R	m	18-21
McGARRAH James	m	10-18
McGARRAH Simpson	No	entry
McGARAH Francis	m	0-10
McGARRAH Mathew	m	0-10

[27]

GRAHAM Nancy	f	16+
GRAHAM John	m	21-45
GRAHAM S	f	16+
GRAHAM Steaphen	m	10-18
GRAHAM Marthey J	f	16+
GRAHAM Wesley	m	0-10
GRAHAM Abitheya A	f	16+
GRAHAM Lucina J	f	0-16
SMITH Laborn	m	45+
SMITH Elvirirey	f	16+
SMITH Rufus C	m	21-45
SMITH Sariceiro S	m	21-45
SMITH Joseph B	m	21-45

SMITH Matilda	f	16+
SMITH Mirah J	f	0-16
SMITH John M	m	0-10
HOLCOMB W H	m	21-45
HOLCOMB Rebeca	f	16+
HOLCOMB Elen	f	0-16
HOLCOMB Carlini	f	0-10
HOLCOMB John	m	0-10
HOLCOMB William H	m	0-10
SMILEY Wm M	m	21-45
SMILEY Alpha	f	16+
SMILEY Joseph H	m	10-18
SMILEY Darthey	f	0-16
LICKLITER David	m	10-18

[29]

LICKLITER William	m	0-10
LICKLITER Marthey E	f	0-16
WHITE Lucy	f	16+
WHITE Sarah	f	16+
WHITE Joseph	m	18-21
WHITE Nancy	f	0-16
WHITE Philomon	m	18-21
BIAS Jessie	m	45+
BIAS Mary	f	16+
BIAS Lizie	f	16+
BIAS Lidda	No	entry
LICKLITER Emley	f	16+
LICKLLTER Elihu	m	10-18
LICKLITER Columbus	m	10-18
LICKLITER Margret	f	16+
LICKLITER William C	m	21-45
STAFFORD Margret	No	entry
NICKLESON John	m	21-45
NICKLESON Margret	f	16+
NICKLESON Darcus A	f	16+
NICKLESON Elen A	f	16+
SMITH W B	m	45+
SMITH Easter	No	entry
SMITH Blake	m	10-18
SMITH Malicia	f	0-16
SMITH John	m	0-10
SMITH Joseph	m	0-10
SMITH William	m	0-10

[31]

SMITH Handa	m	0-10
SMITH James	m	0-10
BAGGET Elizbeath	No	entry
BAGGET Malvina	f	16+

4

BAGGET Marilda	f	16+		HARRIS B G	m	10-18
BAGGET Pelliney	f	16+		HARRIS	m	0-10
BAGGET Abrem	m	18-21		HARRIS	m	0-10
BAGGET A D	m	10-18				
BAGGET Mahala	f	0-16		[35]		
BAGGET Alin	m	10-18		ELM SPRING TOWNSHIP		
STANLEY Martin	m	21-45		AARON Danniel	m	45+
STANLEY Willison	m	18-21		AARON Rachal	f	16+
STANLEY Rebeca A	f	16+		AARON Sirilna	f	16+
STANLEY James F	m	10-18		AARON Winston	m	18-21
STANLEY John	m	0-10		AARON Manning	f	16+
HEAD Elis	f	16+		AARON Bell Z	f	16+
HEAD Amandy	f	16+		AARON Dorinda	f	16+
HEAD K M	m	21-45		AARON James	m	21-45
HEAD Hester	f	16+		AARON Matilda	f	16+
HEAD Marier	f	16+		AARON Abraham	m	0-10
HEAD Hary F	m	18-21		AARON Sithy	f	16+
HEAD Joseph	m	18-21		Amandy	f	16+
FITZGEARLDS J S	m	45+		PEARSON Jacob	m	45+
FITZGEARLDS Jane	f	16+		PEARSON Lida	f	16+
FITZGEARLDS Margret	f	16+		PEARSON Marinda W	f	16+
FITZGEARLDS John	m	18-21		McINRY Jacob	m	0-10
FITZGEARLDS Elisabeath	f	16+		WEBSTER Tho F	m	0-10
FITZGEARLDS Annie	f	0-16		WEBSTER Lizabath A	f	16+
FITZGEARLDS Jane	f	0-16		WEBSTER William T	m	0-10
				WARSON A W	m	45+
[33]				WARSON Hanna	f	16+
FITZGEARLDS James	m	21-45		WARSON Artemissey E	f	16+
FITZGEARLDS John	m	45+		WARSON Josier H	f	16+
FITZGEARLDS Mary A	f	16+		WARSON William D	m	10-18
FITZGEARLDS John	m	21-45		WARSON Alfred W	m	10-18
HARRIS John	m	45+		WARSON D P	m	10-18
HARRIS James	m	18-21		WARSON James F	m	0-10
HARRIS Henry	m	10-18				
HARRIS Samual	m	10-18		[37]		
HARRIS Susan	m*	45+		WARSON Rebeca J	f	0-16
HARRIS Roda	f	16+		WARSON John C	m	0-10
HENSON Joseph N	f*	16+		WARSON Abner G	m	0-10
HENSON E S	m	45+		WARSON Mary	f	0-16
HENSON William W	No entry			WARSON Mary	f	16+
HENSON Mary	No entry			WATERS T H	m	21-45
HENSON S M	f	16+		WATERS Mary	f	16+
LICKLITER John H	m	21-45		BROWN John	m	45+
LIKELITER M	f	16+		BROWN Elisbeth	f	16+
VERNON Samuel	m	21-45		BROWN Sarah	f	16+
VERNON Mary	f	+16		BROWN Hary	m	0-10
VERNON Mary P	f	0-16		BROWN Josiphine	f	0-16
VERNON P F P	f	0-16		BROWN John	m	0-10
GINNES Lipton	m	0-10		HARRIS Buck	m	21-45
HARRIS J E	m	21-45		HARRIS Margret	f	16+
HARRIS Mrs	f	16+		HARRIS Samul T	m	0-10
				HARRIS A F	f	0-16

HARRIS William J	m	0-10
WATERS William	m	21-45
WATERS Abbey	f	16+
BINGEMS B R	m	45+
BINGEMS Nancy	f	16+
BINGEMS Carllotty	f	16+
BINGEMS Nancy F	f	0-16
BROWN Malinda	f	16+
FLEMONS Eliszabeath	f	16+
[39]		
COLLINS Jas Henry	m	21-45
COLLINS Eliszabeath	f	16+
COLLINS Thomas C	m	10-18
COLLINS Nancy A	f	0-16
COLLINS Sarah J	f	0-16
COLLINS William B	m	0-10
COLLINS Jas Henry	m	0-10
COLLINS Bluford A	m	0-10
ESSICKS Isaac	m	45+
ESSICKS Sarah	f	16+
ESSICKS Henry	m	18-21
ESSICKS Hiram	m	18-21
BRADSHAW Isam	m	45+
BRADSHAW Susan	f	16+
BRADSHAW Sarah	f	16+
BRADSHAW Mary A	f	0-16
BRADSHAW Patsey	f	0-16
BRADSHAW James M	m	0-10
BRADSHAW Wm	m	0-10
PHILLIPPS Milton	m	45+
PHILLIPPS Marier	f	16+
PHILLIPPS John (x'd out)	m	21-45
PHILLIPPS Elisabeath	f	16+
PHILLIPPS Wilson	m	18-21
PHILLIPPS Nancy	f	0-16
PHILLIPPS Mary A	f	0-16
SMITH John R	m	45+
SMITH Harriet	f	16+
[41]		
SMITH Polly M	f	16+
SMITH Nancy C	f	16+
SMITH Wm	m	0-10
SMITH Allice	f	0-16
HENRY Jackson	m	10-18
EVANS Margret L	f	16+
SMITH WG WMC	m	21-45
SMITH Herset A	f	16+
SMITH James P	f*	0-16
EVANS John	m	0-10

THORNSBERRY M W	m	45+
THORNSBERRY Telithy	f	16+
THORNSBERRY Walter J	m	10-18
THORNSBERRY Elizabeth M	f	0-16
THORNSBERRY Mary L	f	0-16
_____ Henry	m	45+
DEAVER William	m	45+
DEAVER Sarah	f	16+
DEAVER Mary	f	16+
DEAVER Bingamin	m	18-21
DEAVER David W	m	18-21
DEAVER Jacob	m	10-18
STEEL M D	m	21-45
STEEL Mary O	f	16+
ANDERSON Annie	f	16+
STEEL John T	m	10-18
STEEL William V	m	10-18
STEEL Elizabeath R	No entry	
[43]		
STEEL Thos D	m	0-10
STEEL James C	m	0-10
DEAVER Bingamin	m	0-10
LALE Mary A	f	16+
LALE Armstia	f	16+
LALE Edward A	m	10-18
GIPSON Bethel	m	45+
GIPSON Emley	f	16+
GIPSON Siney	f	16+
GIPSON Milteran	f	16+
GIPSON Sarah	f	0-16
GIPSON Charles D	m	10-18
GIPSON Franklin P	m	10-18
TERRY Thomas	m	45+
TERRY Elizabeath	f	16+
TERRY Rebeca C	f	16+
TERRY Sarah	f	0-16
TERRY Nancy	f	0-16
TERRY Tennisee	f	0-16
TERRY Kimble	m	0-10
TERRY Mary	f	0-16
TERRY S P	m	0-10
NORMON Sinthy	f	16+
NORMON Tho E	m	21-45
NORMON Nancy E	f	16+
NORMON Robt J	m	18-21
[45]		
McCAMA J C	m	45+
McCAMA Nancy	f	16+
McCAMA Marthey A	f	16+

McCAMA Cal Dona	f	16+	
McCAMA Am__a	f	0-16	
McCAMA Pleasant	m	10-18	
McCAMA Thomas	m	0-10	
McCAMA George W	m	0-10	
McCAMA James	m	21-45	
REVIS D D	m	21-45	
REVIS Mary	f	16+	
REVIS Thomas	m	10-18	
REVIS Elizabeth	f	0-16	
REVIS James	m	10-18	
REVIS Sinthey A	f	0-16	
REVIS Harriet	f	0-16	
REVIS Marins	m	0-10	
REVIS William	m	0-10	
REVIS Marthey	f	0-16	
REVIS Margret	f	0-16	
SANDERS K	m	45+	
SANDERS Elzabeath	f	16+	
SANDERS George A	m	18-21	
SANDERS Leanner G	f	0-16	
SANDERS Udoro	f	0-16	
[47]			
DAVIS David	m	45+	
DAVIS Rebeca	f	16+	
DAVIS Elizabeath	f	16+	
DAVIS Samuel	m	18-21	
DAVIS Lucetty	f	16+	
DAVIS Rebeca	f	0-16	
DAVIS Jordon	m	10-18	
DAVIS Lusania	f	0-16	
DAVIS Liveley	m	0-10	
BUCKEY David	m	45+	
BUCKEY Polly	f	16+	
BUCKEY James	m	18-21	
WEBSTER John D	m	45+	
WEBSTER Margret S	f	16+	
WEBSTER Francis	f	16+	
WEBSTER John B	m	18-21	
LOOPER Gilbert J	m	21-45	
LOOPER Sarah A	f	16+	
LOOPER Elizabeath	f	0-16	
LOOPER Ellen	f	0-16	
LOOPER Telithy	f	0-16	
CRUMBEY H V	m	21-45	
CRUMBY Amandy C	f	16+	
CRUMBEY William B	m	0-10	
BRICKEY John M	m	21-45	
BRICKEY Fanny V	f	16+	

[49]			
BUTLER Hudston	m	45+	
BUTLER Susan	f	16+	
BUTLER Lela	f	16+	
ANDREW John	m	18-21	
LOOPER William C	m	21-45	
LOOPER Sarah	f	16+	
LOOPER Gilbert M	m	0-10	
LOOPER Liza J	f	0-16	
BAGGET Isaac	m	21-45	
BAGGET Jane	f	16+	
BAGGET William H	m	0-10	
BAGGET James N	m	0-10	
RITTER James	m	21-45	
RITTER Sarah	f	16+	
RITTER Hugh C	m	10-18	
RITTER Ransom L	m	10-18	
RITTER Newton G	f*	0-16	
RITTER James R	m	0-10	
RITTER Lucy	f	0-16	
RITTER Nancy E	f	0-16	
RITTER Lucinda	f	0-16	
RITTER William R	m	21-45	
RITTER Malinda	f	0-16	
LOOPER Gilbert	m	45+	
LOOPER Emley	f	16+	
LOOPER Benjamin	m	10-18	
LOOPER John	m	18-21	
LOOPER William	m	10-18	
LOOPER Simeon	m	10-18	
[51]			
LOOPER Mary E	f	16+	
LOOPER Bennet	m	10-18	
LOOPER Archey G	m	0-10	
GUTHREY Lawson	m	45+	
GUTHREY Nancy	f	16+	
GUTHREY Liza	f	16+	
GUTHREY Carter	m	18-21	
GUTHRY Annie	f	0-16	
GUTHRY George	m	10-18	
GUTHREY Washington	m	0-10	
GUTHRY Hester A	f	0-16	
GUTHREY Is_on	m	0-10	
GUTHREY Nancy	f	0-16	
GUTHREY Franklin	m	0-10	
WALKER Jessie	No entry		
WALKER Jane	f	16+	
WALKER Mary E	f	16+	
WALKER Wm	m	10-18	
WALKER Jasper N	m	10-18	

WALKER Nancy	f	0-16	McKEE Elizabeath		No entry	
WALKER Marthey	f	0-16	McKINNON Mary J	f	0-16	
WALKER Margeret	f	0-16	McKINNON William A	m	10-18	
WALKER Hester A	f	0-16	McKINNON John P	m	10-18	
WALKER John	m	0-10	McKINNON David F	m	10-18	
COLLINS Sarah	f	16+	McKINNON Abner W	m	0-10	
BARNETT Isaac	m	45+	McKINNON James R	m	0-10	
BARNETT Susan E	f	16+	McKINNON Thomas M	m	0-10	
BARNET George W	m	21-45	McKINNON Marthey R	f	0-16	
BARNET Catherin	f	16+	McKINNON George G	m	0-10	
			COLLINS Martin	m	45+	
			COLLINS Charity	f	16+	
[53]			COLLINS Liza J	f	16+	
BARNET Susan E	f	16+	FORD William	m	21-45	
BARNETT Tennisee	f	0-16	FORD Elizabeath	f	16+	
BARNETT Nancy C	f	0-16	FORD Nancy F	f	0-16	
DOWNING W D	m	21-45	FORD Susan C	f	0-16	
DOWNING Amandy M	f	16+	FORD William G	m	0-10	
DOWNING John R	m	0-10	FORD Lizzie J	f	0-16	
DOWNING Nancy E	f	0-16	FORD Mary E T	f	0-16	
DOWNING Mary F	f	0-16				
FORD Elender	No entry					
FORD William	No entry		[57]			
FORD Malitia	f	0-16	FORD Seltanna E	f	16+	
FORD William W	m	0-10	INGRIM Lewis	m	21-45	
FORD Mary E	f	0-16	INGRIM Mahulda T	f	0-16	
ENNIS Marthey M	f	0-16	INGRIM Marthey V	f	0-16	
ENNIS Isaac	m	10-18	INGRIM Maryan F	f	0-16	
ENNIS Susan E	f	0-16	INGRIM Rebeca E	f	0-16	
QUINTON John	m	45+	INGRIM Harriet E	f	0-16	
QUINTON Allabama	f	16+	INGRIM Charllty T	f	0-16	
QUINTON Sarah R	f	16+	CARTWRIGHT Nancy	f	16+	
QUINTON Mary J	f	16+	CARTWRIGHT George	m	18-21	
QUINTON Julia A	f	0-16	CARTWRIGHT Sarah J	f	0-16	
QUINTON Margret S	f	0-16	CARTWRIGHT William H	m	10-18	
QUINTON Ellender	f	0-16	CARTWRIGHT Beca C	f	0-16	
QUINTON Marier	f	0-16	CARTWRIGHT John R	m	10-18	
QUINTON Drura A	m	0-10	CARTWRIGHT Nancy E	f	0-16	
MAXEY Bradford	m	21-45	CARTWRIGHT Margret E	f	0-16	
MAXEY Selinda	f	16+	CARTWRIGHT JoHanna	f	0-16	
MAXEY Emley J	No entry		MONDAY Rebeca	No entry		
			MONDAY Susan A	f	0-16	
[55]			MONDAY Mary J	m*	45+	
SMILEY Sarah	f	16+	MONDAY James	m	10-18	
SMILEY Sinthy A	f	16+	MONDAY Shelva	m	0-10	
SMILEY Frank	m	10-18	MONDAY Marthey	m*	45+	
SMILEY James	m	0-10	MONDAY Lewis	m	0-10	
SMILEY Henry	m	0-10	McWATERS J B	m	21-45	
SMILEY Dorithey E	f	0-16	McWATERS Catherine	f	16+	
SMILEY Tennissee	f	0-16	McWATERS William P	m	10-18	
SMILEY Hugh	m	0-10	McWATERS Thomas G	m	0-10	
McKINNON George	m	21-45	McWATERS Margret A	f	0-16	

[59]

SHEPARD W C	m	21-45
SHEPARD Nancy C	f	16+
TALLS W F	m	0-10
SONS F	m	45+
SONS Eady	f	16+
SONS Jane	f	16+
SONS Rebeca F	f	16+
SONS Margret	f	0-16
SONS Sarah	f	0-16
SONS John M	m	10-18
WEST A C	No entry	
WEST J C	m	10-18
WEST S E	m	10-18
WEST E E	f	16+
SONS Jas J	m	21-45
SONS Eliza	f	16+
SONS Marien	m	0-10
SONS Narsis	f	0-16
McCOMMOCK Peter	m	45+
McCOMMOCK Chalerrine	f	16+
McCOMMOCK Issablla	No entry	
McCOMMOCK William	m	10-18
RISLEY Wilson	m	21-45
RISLEY Mary	f	16+
RISLEY A	m	0-10
RISLEY Robt	m	0-10
RISLEY John	m	0-10
CASSEY M E	No entry	

[61]

McWATERS Louisa J	f	0-16
McWATERS Loborn H	m	0-10
GRAHAM Ben	m	45+
GRAHAM Elizabeath	f	16+
GRAHAM John	m	18-21
GRAHAM Emiline	f	0-16
GRAHAM Roda	f	0-16
GRAHAM Malicia	f	0-16
GRAHAM Wesley	m	0-10
GRAHAM Margret	f	0-16
GRAHAM Andrew	m	0-10
GRAHAM Susan	f	0-16
PEARSON Saldannar	f	16+
PEARSON William B	m	18-21
PEARSON Sarah E	f	0-16
PEARSON Mary W	f	0-16

MARRS HILL TOWNSHIP

WILSON A J	m	45+
WILSON Ann	f	16+

WILSON Tho J	m	21-45
WILSON Columbus	m	21-45
WILSON Theadore	m	18-21
WILSON Samul	m	10-18
WILSON Harmon	m	10-18
WILSON Wm	m	0-10
WILSON Lee	m	0-10
WILSON Matilda A	f	0-16
WILSON Serena	f	0-16
WILSON Harriet E	f	0-16

[63]

NEAL Dan B	m	45+
NEAL Mary	f	16+
ROBBINSON Mary	f	16+
JOHNSON Alcia J	f	16+
NEAL Isiblla B	f	16+
NEAL Illinra	f	16+
NEAL Bart C	m	21-45
ROBBNSON Dan R	m	10-18
ROBBNSON John	m	0-10
ROBBNSON Abigal	m*	0-10
ROBBNSON James	m	0-10
ROBBNSON Jane B	f	0-16
NEAL Adam	No entry	
NEAL Jeffison	No entry	
NEAL George	No entry	
BORDEN Arch	m	21-45
BORDEN Sarah C	f	16+
BORDEN Ranel B	m	10-18
BORDEN Thomas C	m	10-18
BORDEN Caldona A	f	0-16
BORDEN William L	m	10-18
BORDEN John H	m	0-18
BORDEN Rachal L	f	0-16
BORDEN Julia E	f	0-16
WEST James D	m	21-45
WEST Tregetter	f	16+
WEST Wilford J	m	0-10
WEST Perry L	m	0-10

[65]

DENTON Samuel	m	45+
DENTON Emley	f	16+
JAMES Mary C	f	16+
CATES Caldera	m	0-10
DENTON Sarah E	f	0-16
WEST Tho R	m	21-45
NEAL Emley	f	16+
WEST Arminda	f	16+

9

WEST Umphries	m	10-18	[69]		
WEST Robt	m	10-18	BELL John F	m	45+
WEST James	m	0-10	BELL Hanna	f	16+
WEST Julia	f	0-16	BELL Laura	f	16+
WEST Joseph	m	0-10	COHEE Gilbert	m	45+
WEST Mary	f	0-16	COHEE Margret C	f	16+
WEST Edward	m	45+	COHEE John W	m	18-21
WEST Mary A	f	16+	COHEE Harrit C	f	16+
WEST John M	m	18-21	COHEE James P	m	10-18
WEST Agnis	f	0-16	COHEE Mary J	f	0-16
WEST Thomas	m	10-18	COHEE A N	m	10-18
WEST Elizabeath	f	0-16	COHEE Issblla	f	0-16
WEST Phillipp	m	0-10	COHEE Perry A	m	0-10
WEST William	m	0-10	COHEE C J	f	0-16
EDMISTON Nancy	f	16+	COHEE Annis	m	0-10
DIVEN Mary J	f	16+	LUTRELL William	m	21-45
EDMISTON John	m	21-45	LUTRELL Elizabeath J	f	0-16
EDMISTON Mosses E	m	21-45	LUTRELL Susanna	f	0-16
EDMISTON George W	m	18-21	LUTRELL John H	m	10-18
			LUTRELL Ellender M	No entry	
			PEARSON Nancy J	f	0-16
[67]			CHERRY Joel	m	45+
DIVEN James	m	0-10	CHERRY Mary A	f	16+
DIVEN Nancy A	f	0-16	CHERRY Susan	f	16+
WILSON Samuel	m	45+	CHERRY Isaac	m	10-18
CRAWFORD S R	m	21-45	CHERRY Lewis	m	10-18
CRAWFORD Rebeca M	f	16+	CHERRY John	m	10-18
CRAWFORD Martin L	m	0-10	CHERRY Mary	f	0-16
CRAWFORD John	m	45+			
CRAWFORD James J	m	21-45			
CRAWFORD Rachal	f	16+	[71]		
CRAWFORD William C	m	10-18	COX John M	m	45+
EDMISTON F T	m	21-45	COX Louisa	f	16+
EDMISTON Margret	f	16+	COX Marthey J	f	0-16
EDMISTON Isibella	f	0-16	COX Emiline	No entry	
EDMISTON Samuel	m	0-10	ASHER Walter	m	45+
EDMISTON H R	m	21-45	ASHER Elizabeath	f	16+
EDMISTON Nancy	f	16+	ASHER Thomas J	m	0-10
EDMISTON Laura	f	0-16	PASS Susan	f	16+
EDMISTON John	No entry		PASS Olliver	m	0-10
HINDS Rada	f	16+	ROSE Sidney	f	16+
HINDS R A E	f	16+	ROSE Clementine	f	16+
HINDS W G W	m	18-21	ROSE Dealey	f	16+
HINDS J M K	f	0-16	BROWNLEE W W	m	45+
HINDS C S S	m	10-18	BROWNLEE Marthey A	f	16+
HINDS M J A	m	0-10	BROWNLEE Mary	f	0-16
BELL John M	m	21-45	BROWNLEE Sarah	f	0-16
BELL E C	f	16+	BROWNLEE Henryeta	f	0-16
BELL J C	m	21-45	PASS Susann	f	16+
BELL T M	m	0-10	LUTRELL Sheldon	m	45+
			LUTRELL Louisa J	f	16+
			LUTRELL James P	m	10-18

LUTRELL Samul B	m	10-18
LUTRELL Marthey	f	0-16
LUTRELL Elvin J	m	0-16
LUTRELL Lewis	m	0-10
LUTRELL William M	m	0-10
NEALE W K	m	45+
NEALE Lucinda	f	16+
NEALE Mary	f	16+

[73]

NEALE Robt	m	10-18
NEALE Daniel	m	0-10
NEALE John A	m	0-10
NEALE Grace S	f	0-16
NEALE Charles	m	0-10
PHIPPS James	m	21-45
PHIPPS Trecy A	f	16+
PHIPPS John D	m	10-18
PHIPPS Benjamin	No entry	
PHIPPS Joseph	m	0-10
WELDON Thomas	m	21-45
WELDON Nelley	f	16+
WELDON Henry	m	10-18
WELDON Lurey	f	0-16
LANIGHAM Wm A	m	21-45
LANIGHAM Nancy	f	16+
LANIGHAM Mary	f	0-16
[Enumerator left this line blank]		
EDWARDS George W	m	21-45
EDWARDS John A	m	21-45
EDWARDS Jane	f	16+
EDWARDS William	m	0-10
EDWARDS George W	m	0-10
EDWARDS Americus	m	45+
EDWARDS Sarah	f	16+
EDWARDS Amisdetta	f	16+
SIZMOORE James	m	21-45
SIZMOORE Catherine	f	16+

[75]

SIZEMOORE John W	m	0-10
SIZMOORE Margret J	m*	0-10
SIZEMOORE James	m	0-10
CATE James H	m	21-45
CATE Levina J	f	16+
DICKENSON J C	m	21-45
DICKINSON Lucity	f	16+
DICKINSON Becy E	f	0-16
DICKINSON John W	m	10-18
EDWARDS William C	m	21-45
EDWARDS Elizabeath	f	16+

EDWARDS Malathey	f	0-16
EDWARDS Thomas L	m	0-10
EDWARDS Sarah E	f	0-16
CAVIN William	m	45+
CAVIN Ellen	f	0-16
CAVIN Alaxander	m	18-21
CAVIN Samuel	m	18-21
CAVIN John	m	10-18
CAVIN Margret	f	0-16
CAVIN Marthey E	f	0-16
CAVIN Forgey	m	0-10
CAVIN Mary J	f	0-16
CAVIN James	f	0-10
CAVIN Amburs	m	0-10
CAVIN Allen	m	0-10

[77]

ROSE James	m	45+
ROSE Jane	f	16+
ROSE Nancy A	f	16+
ROSE Sarah	f	0-16
ROSE Tho	m	10-18
ROSE Brunetty	f	0-16
ROSE Samanther	f	0-16
NALLS Rebeca	f	16+
SHORES Verginey A	f	16+
NALLS Sarah E	f	0-16
NALLS John H	m	10-18
NALLS Mary E	f	0-16
NALL Nancy B	f	0-16
NALL Barswell	m	0-10
NALL George G	m	0-10
YAGER Elias	m	45+
YAGER Josefine	f	16+
YAGER Calvin	m	0-10
HOLT Angeline	f	16+
HOLT Elizabeath E	f	16+
HOLT Nancy E	f	0-16
HOLT Mary A	f	0-16
HOLT Amandy	f	0-16
HOLT Rebeca B	f	0-16
HOLT Susan C	f	0-16
BARKER John E	m	45+
BARKER William M	m	18-21
BARKER Margret J	f	16+

[79]
ILLINOIS TOWNSHIP

BARKER Sarah A	f	16+
BARKER Mary E	f	0-16
BARKER Beca C	f	0-16

BARKER Luretta	f	0-16		SMITH Samul B	m	0-10
WASHBURN James	m	45+		SMITH Margret J	f	0-16
WASHBURN Mary	m	16+				
WASHBURN Roda J	f	16+		[83]		
MAY Rannels	m	45+		SMITH Sarah B	f	0-16
MAY Richard T	m	10-18		GIBSON Eliza	f	16+
MAY Hugh C	m	10-18		GIBSON Jane	f	16+
MAY Cora B	f	0-16		GIBSON Amanda	f	16+
MAY John H	f*	0-16		GIBSON Mary	f	0-16
DEANSTAS John E	m	21-45		GIBSON George	m	10-18
DEANSTAS Annie E	f	16+		GIBSON Elizabeath	f	0-16
WINGFIELD W G	m	21-45		GIBSON William	m	0-10
COX John M	m	21-45		GIBSON John	m	0-10
COX May E	f	16+		GIBSON Annie L	f	0-16
COX Charls	m	10-18		SMITH David	m	21-45
TRENT W C	m	21-45		SMITH Elizabeath	f	16+
TRENT B T	f	16+		SMITH Matthew	m	10-18
TRENT M H	f	0-16		SMITH Mude	m	10-18
TRENT E E	f	0-16		SMITH John	m	10-18
RICH William J	m	21-45		SMITH James R	m	0-10
RICH Milley	f	16+		SMITH Sterling P	m	0-10
RICH Henry A	m	10-18		SMITH Peter E J	m	0-10
RICH Harna	m	0-10		BARKLEY Polston	m	45+
RICH Abslum	m	0-10		BARKLEY Rebeca	f	16+
				BARKLEY Eliza J	f	16+
[81]				BARKLEY Mary E	f	16+
RICH Earls	m	0-10		TIMBS John	m	21-45
RICH Emley	f	0-16		TIMBS Louiza	f	16+
RICH James C	m	21-45		TIMBS Wiley	m	10-18
RICH Elika	f	16+		TIMBS Thomas	m	10-18
RICH Robt	m	10-18		TIMBS Marthey J	f	0-16
RICH Rebeca	f	0-16		TIMBS Sarah A	f	0-16
RICH Joseph	m	0-10				
RICH Sanford	m	0-10		[85]		
RICH Margret	f	0-16		TIMBS William	m	0-10
SMITH James	m	45+		PARKS Mary	f	16+
SMITH Rebeca	f	16+		PARKS Walter	m	21-45
SMITH Mathew	m	21-45		PARKS Mary	f	16+
SMITH James	m	21-45		PARKS Samul	m	10-18
SMITH Hanna	f	16+		PARKS Harvy	m	10-18
SMITH Sarah A	f	16+		SHRA Mary E	f	0-16
HERROLD Thomas	m	21-45		SHERA Spate	m	0-10
HERRELD Malvina	No entry			SHERA Matta	f	0-10
HERRELD Charls	m	0-10		PARKS Elvina	No entry	
HERRELD J C	m	0-10		SMITH Jerry	m	21-45
HERRELD Hanna E	f	0-16		SMITH Matilda	f	16+
HERRELD Elizabeath	f	16+		SMITH James	m	10-18
HEARRELD John	m	21-45		SMITH Lizzie	f	0-16
RICHARDSON Matilda	f	16+		SMITH William	m	10-18
SMITH Samuel	m	21-45		SMITH M C	m	0-10
SMITH Nancy J	f	16+		SMITH Harina B	f	0-16

Name	Sex	Age
SHANNON T J	m	21-45
SHANNON J T	f	16+
SHANNON James	m	0-10
SMITH Lizzie	f	0-16
SHANNON Mary	f	0-16
SEAY Columbus	m	21-45
SEAY Sarah W	f	16+
SEAY Joseph H	m	0-10
LITTLE S R	m	21-45
LITTLE Julia A	f	16+
LITTLE Amburs H	m	0-10

[87]

Name	Sex	Age
LITTLE Elizabeath	f	16+
LITTLE Amburs S	m	18-21
LITTLE D W C	m	10-18
SMITH John G	m	45+
SMITH E M	f	16+
SMITH Mary E	f	16+
SMITH A B	m	21-45
SMITH Margret A	f	16+
SMITH Charls	m	10-18
SMITH Emma	f	0-16
SMITH Hannibal	m	0-10
GILBREATH Sinthey	f	16+
GILBREATH Mary J	f	16+
COWEN Wm H	m	0-10
GILBREATH Samuel	m	21-45
GILBREATH L C	f	16+
GILBREATH J E	f	0-16
FINE David	m	45+
FINE A E	f	16+
WALLER Lureta	f	0-16
WALLER Lizzie	f	0-16
BALLARD Thomas B	m	45+
BALLARD Eliza	No entry	
McCOMMOCK Lucinda	f	16+
McCOMMOCK Jinney	f	0-16
McCOMMOCK May	f	0-16
McCOMMOCK Janey A	f	0-16

[89]

Name	Sex	Age
SEAVERS C J	m	45+
SEAVERS Lucina T	f	16+
SEAVERS Ellen L	f	16+
SEAVERS Emma J	f	0-16
BALLARD Marthey	f	16+
BARROUS Jerry	m	45+
BARRES Eunice	f	16+
BARRUS Lewis	m	10-18
SEAGER S C	m	21-45

Name	Sex	Age
SEAGER Sarah T	f	16+
BELL Eliga	m	45+
BELL Sarah	f	16+
BELL Mary R	f	0-16
BELL Zebnier	m	10-18
BELL John	m	0-10
BELL Theodore	m	0-10
WEST James S	m	45+
WEST Jane	f	16+
WEST W P	m	10-18
WEST Marthey A	f	16+
WEST Mary T	f	16+
WEST Eliza A	f	0-16
WEST Nathan T	m	10-18
WEST C E	m	10-18
WEST Mary L	f	0-16
WEST Sam H	m	0-10
JORDON James	m	18-21
JORDON Sereana	f	16+
JORDON Mary A	No entry	

[91]

Name	Sex	Age
JORDON Edward	m	10-18
JORDON Amanda	f	0-16
JORDON Jessee M	m	0-10
MABERRY Polly	f	16+
MABERRY Sarah	f	0-16
CRAIG S A	m	21-45
CRAIG Sarah	f	16+
CRAIG Pleasent	m	0-10
WALKER J S	m	45+
MOORE Jane	f	16+
MOORE Josephin	f	16+
MOORE Mary J	f	16+
MOORE Grizza	f	16+
GIBSON James	m	0-10
MOORE James M	m	45+
MOORE Hannabal	m	21-45
MOORE Elmirey	f	16+
CUNNINGHAM Issobella	f	16+
CUNNINGHAM J H	m	21-45
CUNNINGHAM Eliza	f	16+
CUNNINGHAM John H	m	21-45
MASON D B	m	45+
MASON Elizabeath	f	16+
MASON P P	f	16+
MASON E T	f	0-16
MASON B G	m	0-10
MASON Emma D	f	0-16
MASON Fanney S	f	0-16
MASON D V	m	0-10

[93]				[97]			
REAH Mrs	f	16+		WEST Telithey	f	0-16	
REAH Cab	No entry			WEST Laura A	f	0-16	
[Enumerator left this line blank]				WEST Ann	f	0-16	
NIGHT John	m	45+		WEST Nathan R	m	10-18	
NIGHT George W	m	10-18		HERRELD Isam	m	21-45	
MARYMAN William	m	45+		HERRELD Mary L	f	16+	
MARYMAN Lurana	f	16+		HERRELD William D	m	0-10	
MARYMAN Sinthey	f	16+		HERRELD Jinney	f	0-16	
MARYMAN Jane	f	16+					
MARYMAN Dallies	m	0-10		[97]			
ELELEMS Jones W	m	21-45		HERRELD Tilferd	m	0-10	
ELLEMS Elizabeath E	f	16+		BUSBEY Phillipp	m	45+	
ELLEMS Mary E	f	0-16		BUSBEY Sarah	f	16+	
ELLEMS John W	m	10-18		BUSBEY Tho	m	18-21	
ELLEMS Aldis A	m	45+		BUSBEY Abrem	m	10-18	
ELLEMS Nathaniel	m	0-10		BUSBEY Wm M	m	0-10	
ELLEMS Jones T	m	0-10		BUSBEY John H	m	0-10	
BAITY Nancy	f	0-16		BEATY Alaxander	m	45+	
BAITY Wm	m	21-45		BAITY Francis	f	16+	
BAITY Oliver	m	18-21		BAITY Alvin	m	10-18	
BAITY Puss	f	16+		BAITY Mary	f	16+	
BAITY Sarah	f	16+		BAITY Wm	m	0-10	
GIBSON George	m	21-45		BATTY Catherine	f	0-16	
GIBSON Sally J	f	16+		HOLT D B K	m	21-45	
GIBSON Danniel E	m	0-10		HOLT John D	f*	16+	
GIBSON George W	m	0-10		HOLT Edmond	m	10-18	
GIBSON Julia A	No entry			HOLT Emiline	f	0-16	
				HOLT Mordica	m	0-10	
[95]				HOLT Lenidies	m	0-10	
GIBSON P V	f	+16		HOLT Elizza	f	0-16	
GIBSON Samul	m	21-45		HOLT James L R	m	0-10	
GIBSON Matlda	f	0-16		CARTER Lidda	f	16+	
GIBSON Harnet	No entry			ELLEMS Ruth	f	16+	
GIBSON Grizza	f	+16		CARTER J C	m	18-21	
GIBSON James	m	0-10		RICH A B	m	21-45	
THOMISON Mary	f	+16		RICH Artema	f	16+	
THOMISON T W	m	21-45		RICH Joseph	m	0-10	
MARGNESS T R	m	21-45					
DAVIDSON Alander	m	21-45		[99]			
DAVIDSON Algerana	f	16+		FUNKHOUSER Jacob	m	45+	
DAVIDSON Mary E	f	0-16		FUNKHOUSER L J	No entry		
DAVIDSON John	m	0-10		FUNKHOUSER Bersebey	f	16+	
DAVIDSON Wm	m	0-10		FUNKHOUSER Henry	m	10-18	
DAVIDSON Alvin	m	0-10		FUNKHOUSER Mary	f	0-16	
DAVIDSON Margret	f	0-16		ELLEMS Johnithan	m	45+	
WEST N R	m	45+		ELLEMS Sida	f	16+	
WEST Elizabeath	f	16+		ELLEMS Edward	m	21-45	
WEST Mary	f	16+		ELLEMS James	m	18-21	
WEST Eliz. Matilda	f	16+		ELLEMS Nancy	f	16+	
WEST Elizabeath	f	16+		ELLEMS Mary	f	0-16	

14

ELLEMS Matilda	f	16+	ROGERS L A		m	16+
ELLEMS Edward	m	10-18	ROGERS T F		m	10-18
ELLEMS Tho	m	10-18	ROGERS W A		m	10-18
ELLEMS Marthey	f	0-16	ROGERS J W		m	10-18
ELLEMS James	m	0-10	ROGERS J P		m	10-18
ELLEMS Wm	m	0-10	ROGERS V A		f	0-16
ELLEMS Elizzie	f	0-16	ROGERS Andrew		m	0-10
ELLEMS John M	m	45+	ROGERS C C		m	0-10
ELLEMS Catherrine	f	16+	CARLILE J D		m	21-45
WEST Emley	No	entry	CARLILE M J		f	16+
WEST Mary	No	entry	CARLILE D		m	0-10
WEST Eirey	f	0-16	ROBERTSON Jackson		f	0-16
WEST Mary	f	0-16	ROBINSON Hella		f	16+
WEST Peter	m	0-10	ROBERSON H		m	0-10
WEST Alvin	m	0-10	ROBBINSON Leu		f	0-16
WEST Noah	m	0-10	ROBBINSON Eliz		f	0-16
			ROBBERSON P		m	10-18
			ROBBERSON Mary		f	0-16
[101]			ROBBERSON Wm		m	0-10
DRAKE Wesley	m	45+	ROBBINSON M S		m	0-10
DRAKE Marthey	f	16+	ROBBERSON E		m	0-10
DRAKE P J	f	0-16	ROBBISON Marthey		m*	0-10
DRAKE J W	m	10-18	CATE Obe		No	entry
DRAKE J C	m	0-10	CATE Mary		f	16+
DRAKE F M	m	0-10	CATE S		m	10-18
DRAKE N F	m	0-10				
PARKS J H	m	21-45				
PARKS Catherine	f	16+	[105]			
PARKS W A	m	0-10	THOMASON Mary		m*	18-21
COLLINS Lewis	m	45+	THOMASON J F		m	18-21
COLLINS Sarah	m*	45+	THOMASON Z		m	10-18
KNIGHT Nancy	m*	21-45	THOMASON L J		m	0-10
COLLINS Netia Jane	m*	18-21	THOMASON S D		m	0-10
COLLINS Isabel	m*	10-18	WILLSON B D		No	entry
COLLINS Mary J	m*	0-10	WILLSON Margot		m*	21-45
COLLINS Stanfield P	m	0-10	WILLSON Elzabeth		m*	10-18
COLLINS Mary	m*	21-45	WILLSON Eda Abbegale		m*	0-10
COLLINS Georg	m	10-18	WILLSON Mary A		m*	0-10
COLLINS John	m	10-18	WILLSON Eliza R		m*	0-10
COLLINS Elizabeth	m*	0-10	LIVLEY Wilie		m	45+
COLLINS Lisid D	m	0-10	LIVELEY Eliza		m*	21-45
COLLINS James	m	0-10	LIVELEY R E		m	21-45
ELMS Cynthy	m*	21-45	LIVELEY Nancy		m*	18-21
ELMS Sarrah	m*	0-10	LIVELEY Lorley		m*	18-21
THOMASON J D	No	entry	LIVLEY Malinda		m*	10-18
THOMASON Nancy	m*	21-45	LIVELEY Mary A		m*	10-18
THOMASON William	m	21-45	LIVLEY Harret		m*	10-18
			LIVELEY India		m*	18-21
			Martha		m*	0-10
[103]			LIVLEY James		m	0-10
FARMER W R	m	18-21	LIVLEY William		m	0-10
FARMER J M	m	18-21	ELMS George		m	45+
ROGERS S G	m	21-45				

ELMS Nancy	m*	45+	BRANTLEY William J	m	18-21	
ELMS Thomas	m	0-10	BRANTLEY Allexander	m	10-18	
CARTER Ellen	m*	18-21	BRANTLEY N E	f	16+	
			BRANTLEY John J	m	10-18	
[107]			BARTLEY Dicia	f	16+	
DAVIS James E	No entry		BARTLEY Sarah E	f	0-16	
DAVIS Elizabeth	m*	21-45	GRAHAM Elizabeth	f	16+	
DAVIS J W	m	0-10	MATHEU Disia	f	16+	
DAVIS N E	m	0-10				
DAVIS J S	m	0-10	[111]			
DAVIS J W	m	0-10	MOORE David N	m	21-45	
CABE John	m	45+	MOORE Mary E	f	16+	
CABE M L	m	21-45	MOORE Semanthey A	f	0-16	
CABE J M	m	18-21	ARMSTRONG Hugh	m	21-45	
CABE Mary A	m*	18-21	ARMSTRONG Mary M	f	0-16	
CABE Joseph	m	18-21	ARMSTRONG John T	m	10-18	
CABE William	m	10-18	ARMSTRONG L J	f	0-16	
CABE Jane E	m*	10-18	ARMSTRONG P Wm	m	0-10	
CABE Jacob	m	10-18	ARMSTRONG Abner	m	0-10	
LANE A J	m	45+	WAGNON Baswell	m	45+	
LANE Jonah	m	21-45	WAGNON Mary	f	0-16	
LANE J D	m	18-21	WAGNON Elizabeath	f	16+	
LANE Mary E	m*	10-18	WAGNON Arrabell	f	0-16	
LANE Sarah J	m*	10-18	WAGNON Wm T	m	0-10	
LANE Malinda	m*	0-10	WOODDY Mary A	f	16+	
LANE A J	m	0-10	WOODDY L D	m	10-18	
LANE Thomas	m	0-10	WOODDY Wm	m	10-18	
LANE Daniel C	m	0-10	WOODDY Elley	f	0-16	
YAGAR A	m	21-45	WOODDY Lizzie	f	0-16	
YAGAR Mary	m*	18-21	WOODDY Frank	m	0-10	
YEAR Andrew	m	10-18	MAHEEWS Wm	m	21-45	
YEAGAR Eizabeth	m*	10-18	MATHEWS Ellen	f	0-16	
			MATHEWS E M P	f	16+	
[109]			MATHEWS B D	f	16+	
YEAGAR John J	m	18-21	MATHEWS M J	f	16+	
YEAGAR Sarah J	m*	10-18	MATHEWS D C R	f	0-16	
[Enumerator left this line blank]			MATHEW A B	m	0-10	
EVANS J O	No entry					
EVANS Ann D	m*	45+	[113]			
EVANS L C	m	18-21	MOTTERS John	m	45+	
EVANS W C D	m	21-45	MOTTRES Cire	f	16+	
EVANS Mary E	m*	18-21	MATRES Mary	f	0-16	
EVANS Nathan	m	10-18	MOTERS William	m	18-21	
EVANS M C	f	16+	ROIRTS Solin H	m	18-21	
EVANS J D	f	0-16	WILCOX Elizabeath	f	16+	
EVANS Martha A	f	16+	ROHL E E	f	0-16	
EVANS A D	m	10-18	TOHOMSON Josir	m	18-21	
EVANS J R	m	0-10	THOMSON Dolsono	f	16+	
BRANTLEY E__ls	m	45+	STEVERSON Sarah	f	16+	
BRANTLEY Mary A	f	0-16	THOMSON J C	m	0-10	
BRANTLEY Lawrence W	m	10-18	THOMSON S D	m	10-18	

16

THOMSON D F	m	0-10
THOMSON C M	m	0-10
THOMSON Elizabeath	f	0-16
NORWOOD Mary	f	0-16
COLCLEASAR Jacob	m	18-21
COLCLEASAR Leucina	f	16+
COLCEASARS Hanna A	f	0-16
COLCLEASLER Margret J	f	0-16
COLCOLARE Wealthey	f	0-16
COLCLEASURE Tho J	m	0-10
CARTER David	m	45+
CARTER Mary	m*	45+
CARTER Penelope	f	0-16
CARTER James	m	10-18
CARTER Elizabeath	m*	45+
ROSS Henry	m	21-45

[115]
VINEYARD TOWNSHIP

CHANLER J M	m	21-45
CHANLER Hellen	f	16+
CHANLER William M	m	0-10
GODDARD M L	m	21-45
GODDARD Margret	f	16+
GODDARD William M	m	0-10
GODDARD Dovey	f	0-16
MCLATCHEY J S	m	18-21
MCLATCHEY Ellen	f	16+
JINKINS Loid	m	45+
JINKINS Tho	m	21-45
JINKINS Freman	m	21-45
JINKINS John	m	21-45
JINKINS Emma	f	16+
JINKINS Elizabeath	No entry	
CHANLER Jacob	m	45+
ANDERSON Sarah	f	16+
CHANLER Sarah	f	16+
EWING Young	m	45+
EWING Lucinda	f	16+
EWING John	m	18-21
EWING James Y	m	0-10
EWING Thomas	m	0-10
ALBURTY Sam	m	45+
ALBURTY Sarah A	f	16+
ALBURTY Mary	f	16+
ALBURTY Ufamey	f	16+
ALBURTY Sefornia	f	0-16
ALBURTY Ruthey A	f	0-16
ALBURTY Samuel	m	18-21
ALBURTY Banks U	m	10-18

ALBURTY Dice	f	FPC
ALBURTY Henry	m	FPC
ALBURTY Laura	m*	FPC
ALBURTY Tobe	m	FPC
ALBURTY J C	m	FPC
ALBURTY Joseph	m	FPC
ALBURTY Fred	m	FPC
ALBURTY Viney	m	FPC
ALBURTY Richard	m	FPC
ALBURTY Joseph	m	FPC
LATTY John S	m	21-45
LATTY Fanney S	f	0-16
LATTY Tho F	m	10-18
LATTY John A	f*	0-16
LATTY Margret L	f	0-16
LATTY Mary E	f	0-16
DOUTHET Thomas	m	45+
DOUTHET Sarah	f	16+
DOUTHET Henry A	m	18-21
DOUTHET Wm	m	10-18
DOUTHET Nancy	f	0-16
DOUTHET John	m	10-18
DOUTHET George	m	0-10
ALBURTY Polly	f	16+
HUSE Brant	m	21-45
HUGHES Manervy	f	16+
HUGHES Joanner	f	16+
MARRS Hugh	m	45+

[119]

MILLER Adline	f	16+
MILLER Robt	m	18-21
MILLER Brunettee	f	16+
MILLER Finus	m	10-18
MILLER John	m	10-18
BEASE Rowtt	m	0-16
PATON H J	m	21-45
PATON L T	f	16+
PATON John B	m	0-10
GREER M E	f	16+
GREER J W	m	18-21
GREER T B	m	21-45
GREER M E	f	16+
GREER F A	f	0-16
DENTON G J	m	45+
DENTON Charilty	f	16+
DENTON Bingamin	m	18-21
DENTON Sinthey	f	16+
DENTON Jasier	m	10-18
DENTON Nancy	f	0-16
DENTON Berzelous	m	10-18

DENTON Marthey	f	0-16
DENTON Sarah	f	0-16
DENTON G O	m	21-45
DENTON Madora	f	16+
DENTON Ugene	f*	0-16

[121]

SMITH J M	m	45+
CHANLER Preston	m	45+
CHANLER Mary	f	0-26
CHANLER Lucinda	f	0-16
CHANLER Elizabeath	f	16+

[Enumerator left this line blank]

WASHINGTON G L	m	21-45
IVEY Nathan	m	21-45
IVEY Mary A	f	16+
IVEY Thomas J	m	18-21
IVEY Nathan R	m	10-18
IVEY Rachal	f	16+
IVEY Nancy	f	0-16
BURROW Wesley	m	21-45
BURROW Manervy	f	16+
BURROW Ewing T	m	10-18
CAMBAR Eave	f	0-16
LEWIS A G	m	21-45
LEWIS Catherine	f	16+
LEWIS L J	f	0-16
LEWIS A E	m	10-18
LEWIS C C	f	0-16
LEWIS B D	f	0-16
LEWIS George A	f*	0-16
LEWIS Stelly	m	0-10

[123]

LEWIS G W	m	21-45
LEWIS Mary	f	16+
LONGWITH J M	m	21-45
LONGWITH L M	f	16+
ALBURTY Evaline	f	16+
SHANNON Alaxander	m	45+
SHANNON Sarah	f	16+
SHANNON Marthey	f	16+
SHANNON Mary	f	16+
SHANNON Wm	m	10-18
SHANNON Lawry	f	0-10
SHANNON Jeffison	m	21-45
SIMPSON Harriet	f	16+
LOW Manervy	f	16+
SIMPSON James W	m	18-21
SIMPSON Luciaa R	f	16+
SIMPSON Mary	f	16+

SIMPSON Sarah	f	0-16
SIMPSON Amanda	f	16+
SIMPSON M J	f	0-16
SIMPSON Harriet	f	0-16
SIMPSON Josephine	f	0-16
SIMPSON Henryetta	f	0-16
ISBEY William	m	21-45
McCLAY	m	0-10
LOW Wm J	m	0-10
LOW Fanney	f	0-16

[125]

CHOAT Edward	m	45+
CHOAT Barcila	f	16+
CHOAT Samuel C	m	18-21
EDMISTON D C	m	45+
EDMISTON Rebeca	f	16+
EDMISTON Marthey J	f	16+
EDMISTON E E	f	16+
EDMISTON E T	f	16+
EDMISTON A J	m	18-21
EDMISTON D A	m	18-21
EDMISTON Z B	m	21-45
EDMISTON N J	f	16+
EDMISTON James P	m	10-18
EDMISTON David N	m	0-10
EDMISTON John S	m	0-10
McCLURE George	m	21-45
McCLURE Sarah R	f	0-16
McCLURE Allice	f	0-16
TENNANT Tho	m	45+
TENNANT M C	m	18-21
TENNANT T S	m	18-21
TENNANT J	m	45+
TENNANT Josfine	f	0-16
TENNANT A T	f	0-16
BREEDLOVE W H	m	21-45
BRIEEDLOVE Elmirey	f	16+
BREEDLOVE John W	m	10-18

[127]

GRAY F L	m	45+
GRAY E	f	16+
GRAY M E	f	16+

[Enumerator left this line blank]

BUCHANAN Naima	f	16+
BUCHANAN Ann	f	0-16
BUCHANAN Wiltia	f	0-16
BUCHANAN Naomy	f	16+
BUCHANAN E C	f	0-16
BUCHANAN J T	m	21-45

BUCHANAN A E	f	16+
BUCHANAN Mary E	f	0-16
BUCHANAN Andrew H	m	18-21
BUCHANAN A M	f	16+
BUCHANAN J C	m	0-10
BUCHANAN A B	m	0-10
DAVIS M B	No entry	
DAVIS Tho	m	0-10
DAVIS Albert	m	21-45
SHIPLEY S H	m	21-45
SHIPLEY Sarah J	f	16+
SHIPLEY Mary E	f	0-16
SHIPLEY John	m	0-10
SHIPLEY George	m	0-10
SHIPLEY Samuel	m	0-10
SHIPLEY Ewing	m	0-10
[129]		
MARRS J F	m	21-45
MARRS Marthey A	f	16+
MARRS R A	f	0-16
MARRS George	m	0-10
BURGES Thomas	m	45+
BURGES Nancy	f	16+
BURGES G W	m	18-21
BURGES J W	m	21-45
BURGES Wm A	m	18-21
BURGES Mary	f	0-16
BURGES A J	m	10-18
BURGES Rot	m	0-10
BURGES Nancy	f	0-16
MORROW Hugh	m	21-45
MORROW Harriet	f	16+
MORROW John A	m	0-10
MORROW Hugh A	f*	0-16
MORROW George	m	45+
MORROW Elizabeath	f	16+
MORROW George W	m	21-45
FRESHOUR Henry	m	45+
FRESHOUR Jane	f	16+
FRESHOUR Demsey	m	45+
SMITH Thomas	m	0-10
SMITH Stew W	m	0-10
HUFFMAN Mary J	f	16+
HUFFMAN Harvey	m	0-10
HUFFMAN Emma	f	0-16
[131]		
ENGLAND Elizabeath	f	16+
ENGLAND Joseph	m	10-18
ENGLAND Logan	m	10-18

ENGLAND Darcus	f	16+
ENGLAND William W	m	10-18
ENGLAND C D	m	0-10
ENGLAND George M	m	0-10
ENGLAND S M	m	0-10
MARTIN Issabella	f	16+
MARTIN Wm	m	18-21
MARTIN Mary C	f	0-16
MARTIN Marthey J	f	0-16
MARTIN Sefronia	f	0-16
MARTIN Elmirey	f	16+
MARTIN Mary	f	16+
MARTIN Ewing	m	10-18
MARTIN Samuel	m	10-18
MARTIN Sarah	f	0-16
MARTIN Thomas	m	0-10
MARTIN Sivey	m	0-10
ALBURTY Henry	m	21-45
ALBURTY Henry	m	0-10
ALBURTEY Loransey	m	21-45
BAILES James	m	21-45
BAILES Jane C	f	16+
BALES Adline	f	0-16
GRAY John V	m	45+
GRAY Mary G	f	16+
GRAY Mary E	f	16+
GRAY John C	m	18-21
[133]		
WATERS J M	m	45+
WATERS Emarillers	f	16+
WATERS Vollintinus P	f	0-16
DONIGEN W C	m	21-45
DONIGEN Mary A	f	16+
DONIGEN J H	m	0-10
STEWARD William	m	18-21
SIMPSON George	m	45+
SIMPSON Mary A	f	16+
SIMPSON B J	f	0-16
SIMPSON J M	m	10-18
SIMPSON W H	m	10-18
SIMPSON J L	m	10-18
SIMPSON T J	m	10-18
SIMPSON M T	m	0-10
SIMPSON S D	f	0-16
SIMPSON F B	f	0-16
WRITE Morris	m	45+
WRITE Ruth	f	16+
WRITE Robt	m	21-45
WRITE Morris	m	21-45
MILLER B H	m	21-45
MILLER Laura	f	16+

LEACH Thomas	m	45+	CARNAHAND Mary	f	16+
LEACH Mary C	f	16+	CARNAHAND Marthey	f	16+
LEACH C J	f	0-16	CARNAHAND Elizabeath	f	16+
LEACH T L	f	0-16	CARNAHAND S N	m	18-21
LEACH M F	f	0-16	CARNAHAND Emley	f	16+
LEACH T F	m	10-18	CARNAHAND M V	f	0-16
LEACH A E	m	10-18	CARNAHAND Sarah	f	0-16
LEACH L R	f	0-16	CARNAHAND Press	m	18-21
			CARNAHAND M J	f	16+
[135]			CARNAHAND Stella	f	0-16
FUNKHOUSER Allen	m	18-21	MADARIS W F	m	21-45
FUNKHOUSER T B	f	0-16	MADARIS Lucinda	f	16+
RINHART Margret	f	16+	MADARIS Rot A	m	21-45
RINHART Jane	f	0-16	CRAWFORD J A	f	16+
RINHART M A	f	0-16	MADARIS Wilson F Jr	m	21-45
RINHART Sarah	f	0-16	MADARIS J W	m	18-21
RINHART Wm	m	0-10	MADARIS Tho	m	10-18
HILL Ewing	m	0-10	MADARIS Mary	f	0-16
CRAWFORD Jas	m	45+	MADARIS Wm	m	0-10
CRAWFORD Luvice	f	16+	MADARIS V	m	45+
BLAIR Jain	f	16+	MADARIS Albert	m	0-10
BLAIR E J	f	16+			
LATTY R B	m	18-21	[139]		
LATTY E J	f	16+	CATE F	m	0-10
LATTY M J	No entry		CATE W A	m	0-10
LATTA H T	m	0-10	CATE A J	No entry	
LATTY Frank	m	0-10	MATTERS John	m	45+
SEAY Rufus	m	18-21	MATTERS Eliza	f	16+
EDMISTON Mary	f	16+	MATTERS Mary	f	0-16
EDMISTON Lorena	f	0-16	MATTERS William	m	10-18
BEAN N J	f	16+	ROBBERTS S H	m	21-45
BEAN R H	m	18-21	WILCOX Eliza	f	16+
HERRON William	m	18-21	ROBBISTS E S	No entry	
HERRON S W	f	0-16	WOODROUGH Elizza	f	16+
HERRON Hettsie	f	0-16	ALEN Julo	f	16+
HERRON J M	m	0-10	ALEN Washington	No entry	
HERRON M M	f	0-16	ALEN Mary	f	0-16
NONLEY W A	m	45+	CROFFORD W W	m	45+
NONLEY S A	f	16+	CROFFERD Harett	f	16+
COX M J	f	16+	WILSON William J	m	45+
NONLEY S A L	f	0-16	WILSON Margaret	f	16+
			ROMERY Margaret	f	16+
[137]			GRAHAM Riley	m	18-21
MORROW Georg Robt	m	21-45	GRAHAM Elizabeth	f	16+
MORROW E B	f	16+	GRAHAM Bell	f	0-16
NONLEY Wm W	m	10-18	GRAHAN Tho G	m	0-10
NONLEY F W	f	0-16	GRAHAM William	m	0-10
NONLEY M L	f	0-16	MCASLEN Bethal	m	18-21
NONLEY M E	f	0-16	MCASLEN Wm	m	18-21
NONLEY John A	m	0-10	TINS Eliga	m	18-21
CARNAHAND Samuel	m	21-45	TINS Nancy	f	16+

[141]			EDMISTON Mary	f	0-16	
JOHNSON Robt	m	45+	EDMISTON John	m	0-10	
JOHNSON J W	m	18-21	EDMISTON Florance	f	0-16	
JOHNSON M B	f	16+	MOORE R T	m	21-45	
JOHNSON A E	f	0-16	MOORE Marma	f	16+	
JOHNSON E F	m	10-18	MOORE Marthey	f	16+	
JOHNSON Mary	f	0-16	MOORE Elizabeath	f	16+	
JOHNSON Columbus	m	0-10	MOORE Carline	f	0-16	
JOHNSON Elizabeath	f	0-16	MOORE Catherrine	f	0-16	
JOHNSON Robt	m	0-10	MOORE Laura	f	0-16	
GRISSOM John	m	45+				
GRISSOM Mary	f	16+	**[145]**			
GRISSOM Elizabeath	f	16+	BUCHANAN L J	m	18-21	
GRISSOM Nathan	m	18-21	BUCHANAN M E	m	21-45	
GRISSOM Eliga	f	16+	BUCHANAN Jane	f	16+	
GRISSOM Margret	f	16+	BUCHANAN Suil	m	0-10	
GRISSOM Calvin	m	10-18	BUCHANAN William	m	0-10	
GRISSOM Semanthey	f	0-16	SEXTON William	m	21-45	
YAGAR Benjamin	m	21-45	GRIMSBY Mary	f	16+	
YAGER Lenora	f	16+	LISSENBEE A J	m	21-45	
YAGER Ben	m	0-10	LISSENBEE Sofier	f	16+	
YAGER Wm	m	0-10	LISSENBEE L M	m	10-18	
YAGER F M	m	0-10	LISSENBEE G D	m	0-10	
YAGER James	m	45+	LISSENBEE M E	m	0-16	
YAGER Sarah	f	16+	LISSENBEE A J	m	0-10	
PEAVYHOUSE Abrem	m	21-45	LISSENBEE T J	m	0-10	
PEAVEYHOUSE Elizabeath	f	0-16	REED John R	m	45+	
PEAVEYHOUSE Milicia	f	16+	REED E C	f	16+	
PEAVEYHOUSE Wm E	m	10-18	REED Piolina	f	16+	
PEAVEYHOUSE Marthey	f	0-16	REED Eliza	f	16+	
			REED Wm	m	10-18	
			REED S___yrum	f	0-16	
[143]			REED S___yrum	m	10-18	
MCALEP D R	m	45+	REED Samuel	m	10-18	
MCALEP Sinthey	f	16+	REED Alaxander	m	0-10	
MCALEP C C	f	16+	REED Marthey	f	0-16	
MCALEP Matilda	f	16+	REED H C	f	0-16	
MCALEP John	m	10-18	REED Kizzier	f	16+	
MCALEP Ira	m	10-18	REED Samuel	m	10-18	
MCALEP Mary	f	0-16	REED Ellen	f	0-16	
MCALEP Wm	m	0-10	REED Amanda	f	0-16	
MCALEP David	m	0-10	REED Fanney	f	0-16	
LEACH Nancy E	f	16+	REED _ulina	f	0-16	
LEACH Nancy C	f	16+				
SEAY B C	f	16+	**[147]**			
LEACH Malinda	f	0-16	LARGE Kisire	f	16+	
SIMPSON Hugh	m	18-21	LARGE Tho	m	45+	
SIMPSON Ann	f	16+	LARGE F M	m	10-18	
SIMPSON Lorettie	f	0-16	LARGE Gorge	m	0-10	
SIMPSON Wm	m	0-10	LARGE Prestin	m	0-10	
EDMISTON Wm	m	18-21	MILLER Cirasse	m	21-45	
EDMISTON Elizabeath	f	16+	MILLER Rebeca	f	16+	

MILLER Mary E	f	0-16	BLAKMOORE Sharlott	f	16+
MILLER Henraeta	f	0-16	BLAKMOORE Bell	f	16+
BAIN John A	m	21-45			
BAIN Sarah E	f	16+	[151]		
BAIN John W	m	0-10	RUSSEL J B	m	45+
CATE Elizabeath	f	16+	RUSSEL George T	m	21-45
CATE Allice	f	0-16	RUSSEL Sam P	m	21-45
KEARNS William	m	21-45	RUSSEL J M	m	21-45
KARNES Leucinda	f	16+	RUSSEL Mary R	f	16+
KARNES A L	f	0-16	RUSSEL Wm C	m	0-10
MONGOMERY Jas	m	21-45	CARTER Mary	f	0-16
MONGOMRY Cath	No entry		LACY J M	m	18-21
MONGOMERY Wm	m	10-18	LACY E P	f	16+
MONGOMREY John	m	10-18	LACY Mary E	f	16+
MONGOMREY Harriet	f	0-16	LACY May	f	16+
MONGOMREY Jas	m	0-10	LACY A C	f	16+
DORITY N	f	16+	LACY F H	f	0-16
DORITY E R	m	10-18	LACY Theofelous	m	10-18
DORITY S L	f	16+	LACY Laura T	f	0-16
DORTY Samuel	m	10-18	LACY Allice	f	0-16
COOK M	m	18-21	LACY A E	f	0-16
COOK Margret	f	0-16	PEARSON B H	m	21-45
			PEARSON H W	f	16+
			PEARSON Sarah	f	16+
[149]			PEARSON L A P	f	0-16
REED Allira	f	0-16	PEARSON E J	f	0-16
BARRENS Wesley	m	45+	PEARSON B A	m	18-21
BARRONS Lucinda	f	16+	PEARSON K G	m	18-21
BARRENS John W	m	18-21	PEARSON L T	f	0-16
BARRENS Mary E	f	0-16	PEARSON W E	f	0-16
EARL F R	m	21-45	HANKS N D	m	45+
EARL Amanda	f	16+	HANKS M B	f	16+
BRODIE W B	m	21-45	HANKS John B	m	10-18
BRODIE G A	f	16+	HANKS Mary L	f	0-16
BRODIE Edward	f*	16+			
BRODIE Jane	f	0-16			
BRODIE Elbridge	f*	0-16	[153]		
BRODIE Wm	m	10-18	HANKS Wm D	m	10-18
BRODIE Martin	m	10-18	HANKS N D	m	10-18
BRODIE James	m	10-18	GLOVER H W	m	21-45
BRODIE John	m	0-10	GLOVER Catherine	f	16+
BUCHANAN John	m	45+	GLOVER G B	m	18-21
BUCHANAN Ellen	f	16+	GLOVER Elizabeth	f	16+
BUCHANAN Milton	m	18-21	GLOVER Margret A	f	0-16
BUCHANAN Edward	m	10-18	GLOVER E H	f	0-16
BLAKEMOORE Jessee	m	18-21	KING Wesley	m	21-45
BLAKEMOORE E J	f	16+	KING Joseph	m	18-21
BLAKMOORE Mary	f	16+	KING Earls	m	18-21
BLAKMOORE Sarah	f	16+	KING Hiram	m	10-18
BLAKMOORE Lee	m	10-18	KING Allen	m	10-18
BLAKMOORE Wm	m	0-10	KING James	m	0-10
BLAKMOORE Johnsohn	m	0-10	KING Ben	m	0-10

KING S B	m	0-10	McCOLLOCK Mary T	f	0-16
KING Sarah	f	0-16	CARTER Jas T	m	21-45
KING Mary	f	0-16	CARTER R M	f	16+
KING Emley	f	0-16	CARTER May E	f	16+
HODGES S	f	0-16	CARTER Jas H	m	10-18
HODGES Samuel	m	0-10	CARTER Sarah J	f	0-16
KING Laura	f	0-16	CARTER William	m	0-10
KING Ama	f	0-16	CARTER Laura	f	0-16
DAVIDSON H A	m	18-21	CARTER Corene	f	0-16
DAVIDSON S E	f	16+	CARTER John	m	0-10
DAVIDSON W H	m	10-18	SPENCER Robt	m	21-45
DAVIDSON Abner	m	0-10	SPENCER M C	f	16+
DAVIDSON James	m	0-10	SPENCER L M	f	0-16
DAVIDSON Chestanner	f	0-16	SPENCER John	m	45+
			SPENCER Emley	f	16+
			SPENCER M A	f	16+
[155]			SPENCER John V	m	10-18
McCLELLEND E W	m	21-45	SPENCER Hiram	m	10-18
McCLELAND S J	f	16+	WHITE J S	m	45+
McCLELAND Jo T	m	21-45	WHITE Gemimey	f	16+
McCLLEAND S A	f	16+	WHITE Samuel	m	18-21
McCLLEALAND S G	f	0-16	WHITE Mary J	f	16+
McCLLELAND A C	f	0-16	WHITE F A	f	0-16
McCLLEALAND W P	f	0-16	WHITE James	m	10-18
McCLLEALD L P	f	0-16	WHITE Lizzie	f	0-16
McCLELLAND L C	f	0-16			
DYCHE E C	m	21-45			
DYCHE Mary	f	16+	[159]		
DYCHE Eliza	f	16+	WHITE Allice	f	0-16
DYCHE Leuan	f	0-16	CRAIG Jas S	m	45+
SHARP Wesey	m	16+	CRAIG E A	f	16+
SHARP Richard	m	10-18	CRAIG C R	m	10-18
WILLIAMS W S	m	18-21	CRAIG E A	m	0-10
WILLIAMS Jane	f	16+	CRAIG J H	m	0-10
WILLIAMS Sarah J	f	16+	[Enumerator left this line blank]		
WILLIAMS William W	m	0-10	CRAWFORD F E	m	21-45
WILLIAMS Mary F	f	16+	CRAWFORD Mary A	m	16+
WILLIAMS Hellen F	f	0-16	CRAWFORD Jas E	m	10-18
WILLIAMS Manervey E	f	0-16	CRAWFORD Elizabeath	f	0-16
GREER John D	m	21-45	CRAWFORD Ann	f	0-16
GREER Sarah J	f	16+	SPENCER Isaac	m	45+
GREER Tho C	m	0-10	SPENCER Pinkey	f	16+
COLDWELL Marthey J	f	16+	MOORE Jas	m	45+
COLWELL Dasia	f	45+	MOORE Allice	f	16+
COLDWELL Lucinda	f	16+	MOORE O C	f	16+
			MOORE Bethenie	f	0-16
			MOORE Bell	f	0-16
[157]			MOORE Allice	f	0-16
McCOLLOCK J A L	m	45+	ROSS J M	m	21-45
McCOLLOCK Mary L	f	16+	ROSS J Q	f	16+
McCOLLOCK Clem	m	21-45	ROSS Wm E	m	0-10
McCOLLOCK Mattie	m*	21-45	COMMINGS Francis	f	16+
McCOLLOCK Jurusia	f	16+			

LANKFORD Jas	m	10-18	MABERRY Levy	m	10-18
LANKFORD Liza	f	0-16	MABERRY P S	m	0-10
COMMING Wm	m	0-10	WEAVER Mary	f	16+
COMMING John H	m	0-10	BROWN Wm C	m	10-18
			BROWN W H	m	0-10
[161]			BROWN S R	m	0-10
YATES Lewis	m	21-45	ROGGERS W L	m	21-45
YATES E A	f	16+	ROGGERS Susan	f	16+
YATES Eugne	f	16+	ROGGERS Polina	m*	0-10
YATES Wm N	m	10-18	FOLDEN Jas	f*	0-16
YATES James L	m	10-18	FOLDEN Ridey	No entry	
YATES Edward	m	0-10	FOLDEN Wm F	m	0-10
YATES Clem	m	0-10			
YATES Nicholoas	m	45+	[165]		
REYNELS T A	m	21-45	COX A Y	m	21-45
REYNELS O A	f	16+	COX Sarah	f	16+
REYNELS G K	f	0-16	COX Sarh	f	0-16
REYNELS M L	f	0-16	COX Samuel	f*	0-16
REYNELS To A	m	10-18	CORMACK John	m	10-18
REYNELS Mary E	f	0-16	COX Samuel	m	0-10
REYNELS Johon A	m	0-10	COX Hester	f	0-16
YATES Jas W	m	21-45	COX Marthey	f	16+
YATES M A	f	16+	WELCH W B	m	21-45
YATES Eliza	f	16+	WELCH Laura	f	16+
YATES Jinney	f	16+	HUSTON Jas F	m	21-45
YATES G P	m	0-10	HUSTON Willey M	f	16+
YATES Alta	m	0-10	HUSTON Sarah	f	0-16
BRAWLEY Amanda	f	16+	HUSTON Wm C	m	10-18
BRAWLEY W C	m	18-21	HUSTON T A	m	0-10
BRAWLEY Mary F	f	16+	HUSTON L M	f	0-16
BRAWLEY F C	m	10-18	HUSTON Franklin	m	0-10
BRAWLEY S P K	m	10-18	MABERRY Jacob	m	21-45
			MABERRY Thealder	f	16+
[163]			MABERRY Mary J	f	0-16
CHATEM L E	m	45+	MABERRY Louisa	f	0-16
CHEATEM W T	m	21-45	MABERRY Sarah	f	0-16
CHEATEM J M L	m	10-18	MABERRY Amanda	f	0-16
CHEATEM Mary L	f	0-16	MABERRY David	m	10-18
CHEATEM Elizabeath	f	0-16	MABERRY David	m	18-21
CHEATEM M B H	f	0-16	MABERRY Phenuss	m	0-10
CRAWFORD Susan	f	16+	MABERRY Alley	f	0-16
CRAWFORD Clementine G	f	16+			
CARNAHAN J P	m	21-45	[167]		
CARNAHAN S A	f	16+	RUTHERFORD Archable	m	45+
CARNAHAN A E	m	0-10	RUTHERFORD Sarah	f	16+
CARNAHAN Eva	f	0-16	RUTHERFORD Emberson	m	10-18
CARNAHAN M C	f	0-16	RUTHERFORD Sefronia	f	0-16
CHEATEM G W	m	21-45	RUTHERFORD Amburs	m	10-18
MABERRY Jessee	m	21-45	RUTHERFORD George A	m	0-10
MABERRY B A	f	0-16	RUTHERFORD Leona	m*	0-10
MABERRY Mary	f	0-16	RUTHERFORD Issabella	m*	45+

Name	Sex	Age	Name	Sex	Age
WEESE Henry	m	18-21	COX Burl	m	45+
WEESE Mary	f	0-16	COX Elvirey	f	16+
WEESE Jane	f	0-16			
WEESE Emilin	m*	45+	[171]		
WEESE Carline	No entry		COX Elizabeath	f	16+
WEESE Francis	m	45+	COX L N	f	16+
WEESE Cathernne	m*	45+	COX Ann	f	0-16
WEESE Ellen	No entry		COX C C	m	10-18
WEESE Henry	m	0-10	KERBY H F	m	45+
WEESE Abrem	No entry		KERBEY Jas C	m	18-21
WILLIAMS Isaac	m	21-45	KERBEY Tho H	m	18-21
WILLIAMS Lidda	f	0-16	KERBEY Wm A	m	10-18
WILLIAMS A	f	0-16	KERBEY R A	m	45+
WILLIAMS John	m	10-18	KERBEY A E	m	45+
WILLIAMS Joseph	m	10-18	ENGLISH N P	m	45+
WILLIAMS Marcial	m	10-18	ENGLISH Julia	f	16+
WILLIAMS Col	m	0-10	ENGLISH Sarah	f	16+
WILLIAMS Belzara	m	45+	ENGLISH Volentine	f	16+
STEAVENS Riley	m	18-21	HARBER James	m	21-45
STEAVENS Rachal	f	16+	HARBER Mary	f	16+
STEAVENS Sarah	m*	45+	EDMISTON H H	m	45+
STEAVENS Mary A	m*	45+	EDMISTON Tho	m	18-21
			EDMISTON Jane	f	16+
[169]			EDMISTON John	m	10-18
MABERRY Dacia	m	45+	EDMISTON Elizabeath	f	0-16
MABERRY Nancy	f	16+	EDMISTON Mary	f	0-16
PAIN Margret J	f	16+	EDMISTON Henry	m	0-10
PAIN G E	f	16+	EDMISTON Sarah	f	0-16
PAIN Tho	m	10-18	MITCHEL Mary	f	16+
PAIN John R	m	10-18	MITCHEL Nancy	f	16+
PAIN James P	m	10-18	MITCHEL Alfred	m	18-21
PAIN Marthey T	f	0-16	MITCHEL Mary	f	16+
PAIN Wm A	m	0-10	MITCHEL John	m	18-21
PAIN Margret C	f	0-16			
DRAKE Margret	f	16+	[173]		
DRAKE Malici M	f	16+	HAGOOD Eliza	f	16+
DRAKE J W	m	18-21	HAGOOD Laura	f	16+
SCOTT George W	m	21-45	HAGOOD Hanna	f	0-16
SCOTT Mary	f	16+	HAGOOD George	m	10-18
CROSIER Catherine	f	16+	BATES Henderson	m	45+
CROSIER James P	m	18-21	BATES Ellen	f	16+
CROSIER Arthur	m	18-21	MALOY Mary	f	16+
CROSIER Catherine	f	16+	BATES Lizzie	f	16+
WEATHERSHOON Hanna	f	16+	BATS Margret	f	16+
WEATHERSHOON Cornelia	f	0-16	BATS Annie	f	16+
ISH Sinthey	f	16+	BATS Wm	No entry	
ISH Aullice	f	16+	MALOY Henry T	m	0-10
WEST Crawford	m	18-21	MALOY John T	m	0-10
WEST Arminte	f	16+	MALOY Robt	m	0-10
MARRS Chatman	m	10-18	PYATE Peter	m	0-10
PASLEY Thomas	m	21-45	PYATE Charls	m	0-10

PYATE Finley	m	0-10	BARKER John	m	0-10
NEAL William	m	18-21	PECK A C	m	21-45
NEAL Marthey	f	16+	PECK Nancy	f	16+
NEAL Emiline	f	0-10	PECK B A	f	16+
EDLEMAN Dan	m	21-45	PECK Rachal	f	16+
EDLEMAN Nancy	f	16+	PECK A M	f	16+
EDLEMAN John	m	0-10	KENNON A M	m	21-45
ARMSTRONG Jake	m	45+	KENNON Mary A	f	16+
ARMSTRONG Nancy	f	16+	KENNON George W	m	0-10
ARMSTRONG A James M	m	18-21	KENNON Annie	f	16+
ARMSTRONG Wm	m	10-18	KENNON Charls	m	0-10
ARMSTRONG John	m	10-18	KENNON Dick	No entry	
ARMSTRG Elviry	f	0-16	FORD Mary	f	16+
			BATES Jas F	m	21-45
			BATES Margret J	f	16+
[175]			BATES Clinton O	m	0-10
ARMSTRONG James A	m	0-10	BATES N L	f	0-16
ARMSTRONG J P	m	0-10	BATES Jas H	m	0-10
ARMSTRONG Dock	m	0-10	BATES Wm R	m	0-10
ARMSTRONG Sam	m	21-45	BATS John M	m	0-10
PYATE Wm S	m	45+	BORADEN Margret	f	16+
PYATE Mary	f	16+	BRADEN Henry	m	18-21
PYATE Sarh T	f	16+	BRADEN Mary	f	0-16
PYATE L M	m	10-18	BRADEN Mary	f	0-16
PYATE Orsa O	f	0-16	BARAEN Carline	f	0-16
PYATE Georg F	m	10-18	BRADEN Sarah	f	0-16
PYATE C T	f	0-16	MOORE Lucinda	No entry	
PYATE John	m	0-10			
PYATE Henry	m	0-10	[179]		
WEBBER George	m	0-10	YAGER S N	m	21-45
WEBBER Wm	m	0-10	YAGER E J	f	16+
WRIGHT R B	m	21-45	YAGER George H	m	10-18
BLAKE Samuel	m	45+	YAGER James	m	10-18
BLAKE Marthey	f	16+	YAGER Sias T	m	0-10
BLAKE John	m	18-21	YAGER Eda E	f	0-16
BLAKE Kizzie	f	16+	YAGER B N	m	0-10
BLAKE Liveley	f	0-16	YAGER Redman H	m	0-10
BLAKE Leayer	f	0-16	PYATT Andrew	m	21-45
BLAKE Lizzie	f	0-16	PYATT L J	f	16+
BLAKE Wm	m	0-10	PYATT M C	f	0-16
BLAKE Henry	m	0-10	PYATT W W	m	0-10
BLAKE Coke	m	0-10	PYATT M J	f	16+
BLAKE Wates	m	21-45	PYATT M C	f	0-16
BARKER Jas	m	21-45	PYATT M S	f	0-16
BARKER S A	f	16+	PAYATT Jas F W	m	10-18
BARKER Carline	f	16+	MAPLES E R	f	16+
			MAPLES John E	m	18-21
			MAPLES L A	m	10-18
[177]			MAPLES Wm H	m	10-18
BARKER Jane	f	16+	STEWARDST W J	m	21-45
BARKER Isablle	f	0-16	STEWART Henryettea	f	16+
BARKER Nancy	f	0-16	MILLER E	m	45+
BARKER S A	f	0-16			

26

LEACH Richard	m	45+	RAINEY Catherine	f	0-16
LEACH Jane	f	16+	RAINEY Calvin	m	0-10
LEACH Marthey	f	16+			
LEACH Annie	f	0-16	COVE CREEK TOWNSHIP		
LEACH Semanthey	f	0-16	WOODS Mary	f	16+
LEACH Tho	m	0-10	WOODS George	m	10-18
			WOODS Mary E	f	0-16
[181]			WOODS J W	m	21-45
LEACH Robt	m	0-10	WOODS Marythey	f	16+
PYATT J R	m	21-45	WOODS Mary F	f	0-16
PYATT Elizabeath	f	16+	RINEHART Marthey	f	16+
PYATT Mary A	f	16+	RINEHART Mich	m	21-45
CARNAHAN Mary	f	16+	RINHART Mary E	No entry	
MOORE Wm	m	21-45	WOODS Richard	m	45+
MOORE C N	f	16+			
MOORE Wm H	m	0-10	[185]		
PYATT Henry C	m	18-21	HODGES Howll	m	21-45
PYATT Sarah T	f	16+	HODGES Marthey J	f	16+
BATES P R	m	18-21	HODGES Tho E	m	0-10
BATES Clementine P	f	16+	HODGES M J	f	0-16
BATES James M	m	0-10	CHAMBERS Isaac	m	45+
HAGOOD Adline	f	16+	CHAMBERS Margret	f	16+
HAGOOD Mary C	f	16+	[Enumerator left this line blank]		
HAGOOD Julia	f	16+	CRUSE William	m	21-45
HAGOOD William	m	10-18	CRUSE Marthey	f	16+
HAGOOD Robt	m	10-18	CRUSE Susan	f	0-16
HAGOOD Jim	m	0-10	CRUSE Alaxander	m	0-10
HAGOOD Lizzie	f	0-16	CRUSE William	m	0-10
HAGOOD Mattie	f	0-16	CRUSE Liza	f	0-16
HAGOOD Susan	f	16+	CRUSE Mary	f	0-16
HAGOOD Emley	f	16+	BRUSTER Barsheba	f	16+
HAGOOD Thomas	m	18-21	BRUSTER Hiram	m	18-21
HAGOOD Doke	m	45+	BRUSTER Adline	f	0-16
HAGOOD Liddy	m*	45+	BRUSTER Mary	f	0-16
HAGOOD Lizzie	m*	45+	BRUSTER Marthey	f	0-16
HAGOOD James	m	0-10	BRUSTER John	m	10-18
HAGOOD Gummey	m	0-10	BRUSTER Lafayete	m	21-45
			BRUSTER Elizabeath	f	16+
[183]			BRUSTER Henry	m	0-10
INKS Sarah	f	16+	BRUSTER Ann	f	0-16
INKS Liza	f	0-16	STRICKLER Alfred	m	21-45
INKS Thomas	m	10-18	STRICKLER Mary L	f	16+
WILLIAMS Ira	m	45+	STRICKLER Darcus	f	0-16
WILLIAMS Winney	f	16+	STRICKLER S D	f	0-16
WILLIAMS Marthey	f	16+			
WILLIAMS George	m	10-18	[187]		
WILLIAMS Lithey	f	16+	CRAWLEY William	m	21-45
WILLIAMS James	m	0-10	CRAWLEY Margret	f	16+
WILLIAMS J M	m	10-18	CRAWLEY Steaven H	m	10-18
WILLIAMS Tho	m	10-18	CRAWLEY Marthey	f	16+
RAINEY Nancy	f	16+	CRAWLEY Joseph	m	0-10

1865 SHERIFF'S CENSUS OF WASHINGTON COUNTY ARKANSAS

CRAWLEY Mary	f	0-16	HERRON Nealey	m	0-10
CRAWLEY Lotty	f	0-16	HERRON Emma	f	0-16
CRAWLEY Washington	m	0-10	HERRON Annie	f	0-16
MORROW John	m	45+	RICHARDSON Levy	m	21-45
MORROW Marier	f	16+	RICHARDSON Mirey	f	16+
MORROW Marthey J	f	16+	RICHARDSON John	m	18-21
MORROW George G	m	18-21			
MORROW Margret C	f	16+	[191]		
MORROW Samuel B	m	18-21	RICHARDSON Samuel	m	10-18
MORROW Tho A	m	10-18	RICHARDSON Eli	m	10-18
MORROW James H	m	10-18	RICHARDSON Wilson	m	0-10
MORROW Darcus A	f	0-16	RICHARDSON Franklin	m	0-10
MORROW Emley	f	0-16	RICHARDSON Mary	f	0-16
MORROW Elviriney A	f	16+	RICHARDSON Marthey J	f	0-16
KING Sarah J	f	0-16	STRICKLER Benjamin	m	45+
KING Livianey	f	0-16	BRUSTER Maranda	f	16+
KING Mary A	f	0-16	STRICKLER Albert	m	18-21
STRICKLER William B	m	45+	BRUSTER Marier	f	0-16
STRICKLER G A	f	16+	BRUSTER Navada	f	0-16
STRICKLER Almetea P	f	0-16	BRUSTER William	m	0-10
STRICKLER Danniel J	m	0-10	STRICKLER Samuel		No entry
SIMPSON J B	m	45+	STRICKLER Sarah		No entry
SIMPSON Lucy	f	16+	STRICKLER Barbie	f	16+
SIMPSON Amanda	f	16+	WILHITE Mary	f	16+
SIMPSON Sarah	f	16+	SHARP Marthey		
			WILHITE John	m	10-18
[189]			WILHITE Mary	f	0-16
SIMPSON Mary F	f	0-16	SHARP Lias	m	0-10
RICHARDSON David	m	21-45	SHARP Mary	f	0-16
RICHARDSON Amana	f	16+	BELL Galvest	m	18-21
RICHARDSON Elizabeath	f	16+	BELL Marthey	f	16+
RICHARDSON John W	m	10-18	ADKERSON School	m	21-45
RICHARDSON Wiley	m	10-18	NEAL Jane	f	16+
RICHARDSON Matida A	f	16+	NEAL Minda B	f	0-16
RICHARDSON Eli	m	10-18	NEAL James	m	0-10
RICHARDSON George W	m	0-10	NEAL Carline	f	0-16
RICHARDSON Mark	m	0-10	NEAL Sarah	f	0-16
RICHARDSON Lewis	m	0-10			
HODGES Lewis	m	0-10	[193]		
WHITE Marthey	f	16+	NEAL Marier	f	0-16
WHITE Henry	m	21-45	SCHOOTE Mary	f	0-16
WHITE Jacob	m	21-45	BELL Mary A		No entry
WHITE Robt	m	21-45	BELL John	m	10-18
WHITE Darthey J	f	16+	BELL Porter	m	0-10
WHITE Ellen	f	0-16	BELL Washington	m	10-18
WHITE Hugh	m	10-18	CARL B A	m	21-45
WHITE Salley	f	0-16	CARL Sarah S	f	16+
WHITE Frank	m	0-10	CARL Elbridg D	m	0-10
WHITE Charles	m	18-21	CARL Atlantic N	f	0-16
HERRON George	m	18-21	CARL John T	m	0-10
HERRON Mary	f	16+	CARL Charls R	m	0-10

1865 SHERIFF'S CENSUS OF WASHINGTON COUNTY ARKANSAS

FURGERSON Ira	m	21-45
FURGERSON Charlotte	f	16+
FURGERSON Marthey J	f	0-16
FURGERSON Wm T	m	0-10
FURGERSON Mary E	f	0-16
FURGERSON Hanna	m*	FPC
FURGERSON Lias	f*	FPC
ISAAC William C	m	45+
ISAAC Manervy	f	16+
ISAAC George W	m	10-18
ISAAC Tilman	m	10-18
ISAAC M E	m	0-10
ISAAC Merida	m	0-10
ISAAC Mary M	f	0-16
ISAAC James	m	0-10
ISAAC Edward	m	21-45
ISAAC Henraetta	f	16+
ISAAC Manervey	f	0-16

[195]
MOUNTAIN TOWNSHIP

SAWYERS John M	m	21-45
SAWYERS Mary J	f	16+
SAWYERS John J	m	0-10
DEARNING John M	m	21-45
DEARNING Sarah	f	16+
DEARNING F M	m	10-18
DEARNING G W	m	10-18
DEARNING J S	m	0-10
DEARNING C C	m	18-21
DEARNING Issablla	f	16+
JONES James	m	21-45
JONES Mary A	f	16+
BROTHERTON Ben	m	45+
BROTHERSON Julia A	f	16+
BROTHERTON Mary E	f	0-16
BROTHERTON Marthey A	f	0-16
BROTHERON O C	f	0-16
ASHER John	m	18-21
ASHER Marthey	f	16+
ASHER Tho J	m	0-10
ASER Mack	m	0-10
MORRISON Oliver	m	21-45
MORRISON E T	f	16+
MORRISON William H	m	0-10
MORRISON F M	f	0-16
DYAR F M	m	21-45
DYAR Elisha	m	45+
DYAR Adline	f	16+
BILLINGSLEY Sarah	f	16+

[197]

DYAR Jackson	m	FPC
DYAR John	No entry	
TRUET John	m	21-45
TRUET Manervy	f	16+
TRUET Catherine	f	16+
TRUET Wm R	m	10-18
TRUET Amana P	f	0-16
TRUET Aderiney	f	0-16
TRUET Mary E	f	0-16
TRUET Josier W	m	0-10
TRUET Eliga R	m	0-10
TRUET Leucina B	f	0-16
MORRISON James R	m	0-10
MORRISON Elizabeath	f	16+
MORRISON Annaliza	f	0-16
MORRISON James B	m	0-10
CRAWFORD W D	m	45+
CRAWFORD E C	f	16+
BUCHANAN Tho C	m	18-21
BUCHANAN Mary N	f	16+
CRAWFORD Rachal	f	16+
CRAWFORD Margret	f	16+
CRAWFORD Susan	f	0-16
CRAWFORD Marthey	f	0-16
CRAWFORD Neal	m	0-10
CRAWFORD Lucy	f	0-16
CRAWFORD Emley	f	0-16
CRAWFORD Allice	f	0-16
PHY Harriet A	f	16+

[199]

PHY Hilry	m	10-18
PHY Mary J	f	0-16
PHY Julia	f	0-16
PHY Sile	f	0-16
McCINSEY John	m	21-45
McCINSEY Samuel	m	10-18
McCINSEY Susan	f	16+
McCINSEY John L	m	10-18
McCINSEY A C	m	10-18
McCINSEY Solomon	m	0-10
McCINSEY Wm	m	0-10
McCINSEY Sarah	f	0-16
McCINSEY Aaron	m	0-16
POLK Mary	f	16+
OLIVER Wm G	m	21-45
OLIVER Mary J	f	16+
OLIVER Mary M	f	0-16
OLIVER Sarah T	f	0-16
OLIVER Alzena A	f	0-16

OLIVER Wm A	m	0-10	SAWYERS Josephin		No entry
OLIVER Annie A	f	0-16	SANDERS Steaphen	m	45+
MOCK John	m	21-45	SANDERS Amei	f	16+
MOCK Margret	f	16+	SANDERS R J	f	16+
MOCK James	m	10-18	SANDERS Wm H	m	10-18
MOCK Marthey J	f	0-16	SANDERS Alaxander	m	0-10
MOCK Mary A	f	0-16	SANDERS Mary C	f	0-16
MOCK Sarah C	f	0-16	SAWYRES James R	m	0-10
MOCK Margret L	f	0-16	BLAKEMOORE Tho J	m	21-45
MOCK Josaphen	f	0-16	BLAKEMOORE Emiline	f	16+
MOCK John	m	0-10	BLAKEMOORE Fru Donia	f	0-16
			BLAKEMOORE John	m	10-18
[201]			BLAKEMOORE Lee	m	10-18
STRICKLER Jacob	m	45+	BLAKEMOORE Tho	m	10-18
STRICKLER Malinda	f	16+	BLAKEMORE Jackson	m	0-10
STRICKLER Lucy E	f	16+	BLAKEMOORE Calvin	m	0-10
STRICKLER Elizabeth L	f	16+	BLAKEMOORE James	m	0-10
STRICKLER Benjanin	m	10-18	BLAKEMOORE Hugh	m	0-10
STRICKLER James	m	10-18	MARRS Wesley	m	21-45
STRICKLER Neacy S	f	0-16	MARRS Mary	f	16+
STRICKLER Liza	f	0-16	DEARRING E R	m	21-45
STRICKLER John T	m	0-10	DEARRING Elizabeath		No entry
BUCHANAN Siney	f	16+			
NEAL Lucy J	f	16+	[205]		
NEAL Andrew B	m	10-18	DEARRING James H	m	10-18
NEAL William T	m	10-18	DEARRING E J	f	0-16
NEAL Hugh T	m	10-18	DEARRING Narsis	f	0-16
NEAL Joel P	m	0-10	DEARRING John W	m	10-18
NEAL Annaliza	f	0-16	DEARRING Arrazona	f	0-16
COCKNIM O M	m	21-45	DEARRING Mary	f	0-16
BAKER Richmond	m	21-45	DEARRING Sarah	f	0-16
BAKER Mary E	f	16+	BARRON H H	m	21-45
BAKER Ada A	f	0-16	BARRON Dicy	f	0-16
HANCOCK Robt	m	45+	BARRON George H	m	10-18
HANCOCK Sarah J	f	16+	BARRON Gus	m	10-18
HANCOCK Marthey	f	16+	BARRON Lewis E	m	0-10
HANCOCK Nancy C	f	16+	BARRON Sarah A	f	0-16
HANCOCK Ben A	m	10-18	BARRON Marthey S	f	0-16
HANCOCK Julia A	f	0-16	HOLLAND John	m	21-45
HANCOCK Wm G	m	10-18	HOLLAND Louisa	f	16+
HANCOCK Elizabeath	f	0-16	HOLLAND Rubin	m	10-18
CAVIN John L	m	21-45	HOLLAND Nancy	f	0-16
			HOLLAND William	m	10-18
[203]			HOLLAND Adline	f	0-16
SAWYERS Robt A	m	45+	HOLLAND Franklin	m	0-10
SAWYERS R C	f	16+	HOLLAND Wiley	m	0-10
SAWYERS S E	f	16+	VANCE Mary A	f	0-16
SAWYERS Siney A	f	0-16	VANCE Hanna	f	0-16
SAWYERS M L	f	0-16	VANCE Telithey	f	16+
SAWYERS Mary C	f	0-16	VANCE Sarah	f	16+
SAWYERS Lucinda M	f	0-16	VANCE William J	m	10-18

VANCE Lucinda	f	0-16	ANDERSON Sarah V	f	0-16
VANCE Mary J	f	0-16	ANDERSON G B	m	21-45
			ANDERSON S G	f	16+
[207]			ANDERSON Catherin	f	0-16
VANCE Andrew	m	0-10	ANDERSON William	m	10-18
VANCE Mary A	f	0-16	ANDERSON C F	m	10-18
VANCE Jessee	m	0-10	JORDON Jessee	m	21-45
HOW Young	f	0-16	JORDON Elizabath	f	16+
[Enumerator left this line blank]			JORDON John A	m	18-21
HOWEL W B	m	45+	JORDEN Nancy	f	16+
HOWEL Malinda	f	16+	JORDEN Jessee J M	m	10-18
HOWEL Amanda	f	16+	JORDEN Newton S	f*	0-16
HOWEL James	m	10-18	JORDEN Mary	f	0-16
HOWEL Mirum	f	0-16	JORDON Christopher	m	0-10
HOWEL Wilbern D	m	10-18			
RIEFF Taneris	m	45+	[211]		
RIEFF Charlotey	f	16+	JORDON O D C	m	0-10
RIEFF Brunetty J	f	16+	JORDON Jeffeson	m	0-10
RIEFF Francis M	m	18-21	RUTHERFORD W B	m	21-45
RIEFF Mary L	f	16+	RUTHERFORD Nancy M	f	16+
RIEFF George W	m	10-18	RUTHERFORD Harrret N	f	0-16
RIEFF Lemuel T	m	21-45	RUTHERFORD John F	m	0-10
RIEFF John H	m	21-45	RUTHERFORD Robt L	m	0-10
RIEFF Mary A	f	16+	RUTHERFORD Marier	f	16+
RIEFF Mastin L	m	10-18	GILBREATH S D	m	18-21
RIEFF Lucy A	f	0-16	GILBREATH Susan M	f	16+
RIEFF Elizabeath R	f	0-16	GRAHAM Albert	m	0-10
RIEFF V H T	f	0-16	SHARP R A	m	21-45
LEWIS Elizabeath B	f	16+	BARRON Joseph	m	45+
LEWIS Walker	m	10-18	BARRON Flemmon	f	16+
LEWIS Claborn	m	10-18	BARRON James M	m	18-21
LEWIS Wilson	m	10-18	BARRON John A	m	21-45
LEWIS Mary	f	0-16	BARRON Mary J	f	16+
			BARRON Wm G	m	0-10
[209]			BARRON E H	m	0-10
LEWIS Margret	f	0-16	BILLINGSLEY John	m	45+
TANKERSLEY James A	m	21-45	TANKERSLEY O D	m	21-45
TANKERSLEY Cerenia	f	16+	TANKERSLEY Sarah E	f	16+
TANKERSLEY Samuel G	m	10-18	TANKERSLEY Marthey A	f	0-16
TANKERSLEY Francis S	f	16+	TANKERSLEY Mary E	f	0-16
WHITE John C	m	21-45	TANKERSLEY Susan A	f	0-16
WHITE Cleranda	f	16+	GRIGREY Few	m	21-45
WHITE James B	m	0-10	GRIGREY Easter	f	0-16
WHITE M A	f	0-16	GRIGREY A B	m	21-45
WHITE Marthey J	f	0-16	GRIGREY William	m	21-45
ANDERSON W D	m	45+	GRIGREY Fanney	f	0-16
ANDERSON Julia V	f	16+			
ANDERSON John	m	10-18	[213]		
ANDERSON Charl	m	10-18	LATHREYM Wm	m	45+
ANDERSON Mary J	f	0-16	LATHREYM Pheba	f	16+
ANDERSON James	m	0-10	LATHREM Sarah E	f	16+

31

Name	Sex	Age		Name	Sex	Age
RUTHERFORD John W	m	21-45		GRIGREY Jane	f	16+
RUTHERFORD Mary J	f	16+		GRIGREY Margret	f	16+
BUCHANAN Leander	m	45+		GRIGREY James	m	10-18
BUCHANAN Margey	f	16+		GRIGREY Henry	m	0-10
BUCHANAN Ellen	f	16+		GRIGREY Tho	m	0-10
BUCHANAN John	m	21-45				
BUCHANAN Cassander	f	16+		[217]		
BUCHANAN Wm L	m	0-10		GRIGREY Price	m	0-10
CRAWFORD Marthey	f	16+		WHEALER B H	m	21-45
PYATT Sarah	f	16+		WHEALER Mahala	f	16+
PYATT Miere	f	16+		WHEALER Francis	f	0-16
CRAWFORD Tho	m	0-10		WHEALER Annie	f	0-16
CRAWFORD John	m	0-10		PETIGREW J M	m	45+
CRAWFORD Andrew	m	0-10		PETIGREW M J	f	16+
SIMPSON William	m	18-21		PETIGREW Sarah A	f	16+
PYATT Richard	m	21-45		PETIGREW Charls A	m	10-18
TANKERSLEY Larkin	m	45+		MARION Henry C	m	0-10
TANKERSLEY Thealey	f	16+		BUCHANAN Marthey	f	16+
TANKERSLEY Elizabeath	f	16+		GRAY Salley	f	16+
TANKERSLEY Catherrine	f	16+		GRAY Marthey	f	0-16
TANKERSLEY Lenard	m	21-45		GRAY Allice	f	0-16
TANKERSLEY Cambple G	m	18-21		GRAY Clementine	f	0-16
TANKERSLEY Mary J	f	16+		CROUCH Mary	f	16+
TANKERSLEY Millared	f	0-16		COUCH Ewing	m	10-18
NOLEN G B	m	45+		COUCH Allice	f	16+
NOLEN Elizabeath	f	16+		COUCH Jinney	f	0-16
				COUCH Annie	f	0-16
[215]				PARKS W B	m	18-21
BENSON J A	f	16+		PARKS N J	f	16+
NOLEN Mary E	f	16+		PARKS Adison A	m	0-10
MILLER George	m	45+		PARKS Mary E	f	0-16
MILLER Nancy	f	16+		PARKS T J	f	0-16
MILLER Rebeca	f	0-16		PARKS J B	m	0-10
MILLER Samuel B	m	10-18				
MILLER James	m	10-18		[219]		
HANNA Marthey	f	16+		SMITH Mary	f	16+
HANNA Marthey	f	16+		SMITH Sarah L	f	16+
HANNA Sarah	f	0-16		SMITH James	m	21-45
HANNA James	m	10-18		REES William	m	45+
HANNA Permelia	f	0-16		REES L J	f	16+
YOUNG J M	m	45+		REES Margret	f	16+
YOUNG Mary A	f	16+		REES Tho	m	10-18
YOUNG Harriet N	f	16+		CARNEY Joseph	m	45+
YOUNG Nancy J	f	0-16		CARNEY Peonelope	f	16+
YOUNG Ewing	m	0-10		CARNEY John L	m	10-18
YUNG James E	m	0-10		WEST R J	m	45+
WEBBER Mary J	f	0-16		WEST Julia A	f	16+
GRIGREY Phillipp	m	45+		WEST Mary J	f	0-16
GRIGREY Wm	m	21-45		WEST Margret	f	0-16
GRIGREY George L	m	21-45		WEST Clementine	f	0-16
GRIGREY Marandey	f	16+		WEST Josphen	f	0-16

WEST Passia	f	0-16	HARRISON R M		f	16+
CARROL John	m	45+	HARRISON R P		m	21-45
CARROL Julia A	f	16+	HARRISON Mary E		f	16+
CARROL John R	m	0-10	SHARP Mary		f	16+
CARROL James H	m	0-10	SHANNON John		m	10-18
CARROL Elis	m	0-10	SHANNON Samuel D		m	10-18
CIMES Susan	f	16+	SHANNON James M		m	0-10
CIMES Wm	m	10-18	HULSE Isaac		m	18-21
CIMES Mary	f	0-16	HULSE Margret M		f	16+
CARROL F M	m	21-45	HULSE John		m	0-10
RUTHERFORD N G	f	0-16	HULSE Sarah J		f	16+
RUTHERFORD Elizabeath	f	16+	HOLCOMB William		m	45+
CAMBLLE John	m	18-21	HOLCOMB Sarah		f	16+
			HOLCOMB George P		m	18-21
[221]			HOLCOMB John W		m	18-21
CAMBPLES Malicia	f	16+	HOLCOMB Wm J		m	10-18
TINNEN Harriet	f	16+	HOLCOMB Wilson Z		m	10-18
WHITSET Francis	f	0-16	HOLCOMB Joseph		m	10-18
WHITSET John	m	10-18	HOLCOMB Tho		m	0-10
WHITSET Harriet	f	0-16	HOLCOMB Sarah E		f	0-16
RUTHERFORD Balis	m	45+	JONES Jas F		m	45+
RUTHERFORD Mary	f	16+	JONES Louisa		f	16+
RUTHERFORD Elizabeath	f	0-16	JONES John W		m	18-21
RUTHERFORD Wm	m	10-18	JONES Emberson		m	18-21
RUTHERFORD Calvin	m	10-18				
RUTHERFORD John	m	0-10	[225]			
RUTHERFORD James	m	0-10	JONES Sarah A		f	16+
RUTHERFORD Marthey J	f	0-16	JONES Hiley		f	16+
RUTHERFORD Nol	m	0-16	JONES David		m	18-21
RUTHERFORD Balis	m	0-10	JONES Abrem		m	10-18
MALICOAT Dedmon	m	45+	JONES Nelson		m	10-18
MALICOAT Nancy	f	16+	JONES Clementine		f	0-16
MALICOAT N J	f	0-16	JONES Wilson		m	0-10
MALICOAT Nelson	m	10-18	JONES Marthey		f	0-16
MALICOAT Jane	f	16+	MALLICOAT Cammellon		m	21-45
MALICOAT Elizabeath	f	0-16	MALLICOAT Nancy L		f	16+
DYAR J S	m	21-45	MALLICOAT Mary E		f	0-16
DYAR L C	f	16+	MALLICOAT Sarah E		f	0-16
DYAR M E	f	0-16	MALLICOAT John H		m	0-10
DYAR M A	f	0-16	MALLICOAT Marthey J		f	0-16
DYAR L H	m	10-18	SAWYERS Henry A		m	21-45
DYAR Sarah A	f	0-16	SAWYERS Mary E		f	16+
GUTHREY John	m	45+	JONES Thomas		m	45+
GUTHEREY James	m	10-18	JONES Elisabeth		f	16+
			JONES Manurva		f	16+
[223]			JONES Lucinda		f	16+
GUTHREY John D	m	10-18	JONES Luisa		f	0-16
GUTHREY Elisha	m	0-10	JONES Rosanna		f	0-16
GUTHREY Sarah	f	0-16	JONES Thomas		m	10-18
GUTHREY Henry	m	0-10	JONES William		m	10-18
HARRISON G L	m	45+	JONES Delcna		m	10-18

33

JONES Alfred B	m	45+		HOWEL Suck	f	FPC
CAVIN Annias	m	45+		SAWYERS Lear	f	FPC
CAVIN Mary	f	16+		SAWYERS Sinthey	f	FPC
CAVIN Lewis J	m	18-21		BLAKEMOORE Bud	f	FPC
				CAVIN James	m	21-45
[227]				CAVIN Matilda	f	16+
CAVIN Sarah Margret	f	16+		OWENS James	m	10-18
CAVIN W B	m	10-18		OWENS Sarah J	f	0-16
CAVIN Mary E	f	0-16		CAVIN Wm	m	0-10
CAVIN Adline	f	0-16		OWENS Danel	m	45+
CAVIN Martha	m*	0-10		HOW Ama	f	16+
CAVIN Andrew	m	0-10		HOW Betty	f	0-16
DICKSON A	m	21-45		HOW Jacob	m	18-21
DICKSON C A	f	16+		BUTTS Elizabeath	f	16+
SAWYERS James M	m	45+				
SAWYERS Leucinda	f	16+		[231]		
SAWYERS A K	m	18-21		MORRISON Joseph	m	45+
SAWYERS Alonzo	m	10-18		MORRISON Phebe	f	16+
CARTER Adam	m	21-45		MORRISON M E	f	16+
CARTER Mary M	f	16+		MORRISON Mary C	f	16+
DODSON Mirum	f	16+		MORRISON Jane N	f	16+
DODSON Wesley	m	FPC		MORRISON Nancy E	f	16+
DODSON Cloley	f	FPC		MORRISON Marthey A	f	0-16
DODSON Amanda	f	FPC		MORRISON Harriet A	f	0-16
DODSON Fanney	f	FPC		MORRISON Josephen	f	0-16
DODSON Mary	f	FPC		MORRISON Alaxander	m	0-10
DODSON John	f*	FPC		MORRISON Ophelia	f	0-16
DODSON Lucy	f	FPC		MORRISON D W L	m	0-10
RUTHERFORD Isaac	m	FPC		TANKERSLEY S G	m	21-45
RUTHERFORD Salley	f	FPC		TANKERSLEY Manervy	f	16+
RUTHERFORD James	m	FPC		TANKERSLEY E D	m	10-18
RUTHERFORD Joseph	m	FPC		TANKERSLEY M A	f	0-16
RUTHERFORD Samuel	m	FPC		TANKERSLEY Frace L	m	0-10
RUTHERFORD Mary	f	FPC		TANKERSLEY Mary A	f	0-16
RUTHERFORD Luke	m	FPC		CARNEY Thomas	m	45+
				CARNEY Annie	f	16+
[229]				CARNEY Tennisee	f	16+
DODSON Isaac	m	FPC		CARNEY Margret	f	16+
DODSON Emiline	f	FPC		CARNEY Henson M	m	10-18
DODSON Lucy	f	FPC		CARNEY Thomas J	m	10-18
RATHER John	m	21-45		CARNEY William G	m	0-10
RATHER Lucinda	f	16+		CARNEY Mary B	f	0-16
RATHER Dicey	f	16+		HILL Elizabeath	f	16+
RATHER Francis	f	0-16		CRUSE Mary	f	0-16
RATHER George	m	10-18		HILL Wilbern	m	21-45
RATHER James D	f*	0-16				
RATHER Kissey	f	0-16		[233]		
SHANNON Green	m	FPC		CARNEY Jas W	m	45+
SHANNON David	m	FPC		CARNEY Nancy	f	16+
HOWEL Peter	m	FPC		CARNEY Henry T	m	21-45
HOWEL Hugh	m	FPC		CARNEY George G	m	21-45

CARNEY William J	m	21-45
CARNEY Arthur E	m	18-21
CARNEY John T	m	10-18
CARNEY Lucinda M	f	0-16
RUTHERFORD John A	m	45+
RUTHERFORD Elizabeath	f	16+
RUTHERFORD Joseph	m	10-18
RUTHERFORD Mary	f	16+
RUTHERFORD Calvin	m	0-10
WEST FORK TOWNSHIP		
WINN Eli	No	entry
WINN Matilda F	f	16+
WINN Thomas	m	10-18
WINN Leurina	f	0-16
WINN Sarah	f	0-16
WINN James	m	0-10
WINN Nancy	f	0-16
CURTIS F F	m	21-45
CURTIS N J	f	16+
CURTIS G A	m	0-10
CURTIS B F	m	0-10
CURTIS E E	f	0-16
CURTIS John S	m	0-10
SMEDLEY G E	m	21-45
SMEDLEY Ruth	f	16+
[235]		
SMEDLEY Mary	f	0-16
CRAWFORD Arthur	m	45+
CRAWFORD Sarah	f	16+
CRAWFORD Johnson	m	18-21
PANTER Mary	f	16+
CRAWFORD Adline	f	16+
CRAWFORD Susan A	f	0-16
CRAWFORD Sarah	f	0-16
PANTER Cidney	f	0-16
FURGERSON A	m	18-21
BLOYD Peter	m	45+
BLOYD Sarah	f	16+
BLOYD John	m	10-18
BLOYD Henry	m	0-10
BLOYD Mary	f	16+
BLOYD Lucinda	f	16+
PURSER Peter	m	45+
PURSER Louisa	f	16+
PURSER Marthey	f	16+
PURSER Mary	f	16+
PURSER Charity	f	0-16
PURSER Sarah	f	0-16
PURSER Peter	m	0-10

PURSER Harriet	f	0-16
PURSER Morgin	m	0-10
HEAD H F	m	21-45
HEAD Sarah	No	entry
HEAD M P	f	0-16
HEAD Joseph E	m	0-10
HEAD A S	f	0-16
[237]		
LOFTEN J A	m	21-45
LOFTEN Margret	f	16+
LOFTEN Matilda	f	16+
LOFTEN Dines	m	10-18
LOFTEN Wm R	m	0-10
LOSTEN Jas B	m	0-10
LOFTEN Lucinda	f	0-16
LOFTEN Mindey	f	0-16
LOFTEN Jane	f	16+
WOODS John D	m	21-45
WOODS Sarah	f	16+
GRAHAM John	m	45+
GRAHAM Emiline	f	16+
GRAHAM Wilson	m	21-45
GRAHAM Cirus	m	10-18
GRAHAM Wilbern D	m	10-18
GRAHAM Peter	m	21-45
GRAHAM Narsis	f	16+
GRAHAM Sarah E	f	0-16
GRAHAM Wilson	m	0-10
LITTLE B F	m	21-45
MAILES A C	m	21-45
MALES Elizabeath	f	16+
MAILES Archable	m	10-18
MAILES Francis	m	10-18
MAILES Prudence J	f	0-16
EVANS Nancy	f	0-16
STOCKBUGAR J C	m	21-45
STOCKBUGAR M A	m	10-18
STOCKBUGAR J W	m	10-18
STOCKBUGAR John	m	10-18
[239]		
STOCKBUGAR Nancy	f	0-16
STOCKBUGAR Annie	f	0-16
STOCKBUGAR Joseph	m	0-10
STOCKBUGAR Mary	f	0-16
FINE Wm B	m	45+
FINE Spencer	m	21-45
FINE Henry	m	21-45
Sarah	No	entry
FINE Zacrier	m	18-21

1865 SHERIFF'S CENSUS OF WASHINGTON COUNTY ARKANSAS

Name	Sex	Age		Name	Sex	Age
FINE Lewis	m	10-18		WINN Marthey A	f	0-16
FINE Bluford	m	10-18				
FINE Samuel	m	10-18		[243]		
FINE Mary	f	0-16		WINN Walker	m	0-10
FINE Adline	f	0-16		WINN Emiline	f	FPC
STOCKBUGAR Marthey A	f	16+		KARNES Andrew	m	45+
FINE Milley	f	16+		KARNES Liza	f	16+
LITTLE John	m	45+		KARNES Sianey	f	16+
LITTLE Margret	f	16+		KARNES Phelix G	m	18-21
LITTLE Lucy	f	16+		WOLSEY Wm T	m	45+
LITTLE Rebeca	f	16+		WOLSEY Charity	f	16+
LITTLE Permeley	f	16+		WOLSEY Marthey	f	16+
LITTLE Marthey	f	0-16		WOLSEY John	m	10-18
LITTLE Mary	f	0-16		WOLSEY Charity W	f	0-16
LITTLE Nancy	f	0-16		REED James	m	18-21
LITTLE Mark	m	10-18		KARNES Danniel	m	21-45
LOUDON W P	m	21-45		KARNES Rachal	f	16+
LOUDON Rebeca	f	16+		KARNES George	m	0-10
LOUDON Jessee E	m	0-10		KARNES James	m	0-10
LOUDON John L	m	0-10		STRICKLEN Cidney	f	0-16
SINKLER Elizabeath	f	16+		STRICKLEN Jeraney	f	0-16
				STRICKLEN Charles	m	18-21
[241]				WINN Zadock	m	21-45
HUTCHENS Aquiler	m	45+		WINN Mary A	f	16+
HUTCHENS Winney	f	16+		WINN Melvina	f	0-16
HUTCHENS Liza	f	0-16		WINN Nancy	f	0-16
HUTCHENS Aquiler	m	10-18		WINN Matilda	f	0-16
HUTCHENS Elcaney	m	0-10		WINN William	m	0-10
HARP A J	m	21-45		WINN Leucinda	f	0-16
HARP Sarah J	f	16+		CAUGHMAN Alfred	m	21-45
HARP Tho J	m	0-10		CAUGHMAN Rachal	f	16+
HARP Mary E	f	0-16		CAUGHMAN Nathan	m	18-21
HARP L F	f	0-16		CAUGHMAN Louisa	f	0-16
HARP Sarah A	f	0-16				
KARNES John	m	21-45		[245]		
KARNES Rachal	f	16+				
KARNES Jas A	m	0-10		CAUGHMAN Lurinda	f	0-16
KARNES Henry L	m	0-10		CAUGHMAN Mary J	f	0-16
WINN Z C	No entry			CAUGHMAN Matilda	f	0-16
WINN Marinda	f	16+		CAUGHMAN Nathan	m	45+
WINN Adline	f	0-16		CAUGHMAN Matilda	f	16+
WINN Catherine	f	0-16		CAUGHMAN Nancy A	f	0-16
WINN Nancy E	f	0-16		ANDERSON Tho	m	0-10
WINN James	m	45+		PETERS Aaron	m	45+
WINN Liza	f	16+		PETERS Marthey	f	16+
WINN John	m	18-21		PETERS Jacob	m	10-18
WINN Mary	f	16+		PETERS James	m	10-18
WINN Sinthey	f	0-16		ANDERSON A C	m	21-45
WINN Joel	m	10-18		ANDERSON Jane	f	0-16
WINN Eamoney	f	0-16		ANDERSON Sarah	f	0-16
WINN Margret	f	0-16		ANDERSON Kizzie	f	0-16

ANDERSON Clearisey	f	0-16	NOTT Sarah W	f	0-16
GILBREATH C G	f	0-16	NOTT Francis M	m	10-18
GILBREATH H W	f	0-16	RAIMMY Pheba	f	0-16
GILBREATH Syntha	f	16+	TAYLOR Wm	m	21-45
GILBREATH Margat	No entry		TAYLOR Sarah	f	16+
BLOYD Martha	f	16+	TAYLOR Mary J	f	0-16
GILBREATH William	m	10-18	NOTT John	m	21-45
GILBREATH Cyrus	m	0-10	NOTT Sarah	f	0-16
GILBREATH Antonia	No entry		NOTT Mineysta	f	0-16
KARNES Lafayete	m	21-45	HUTCHENS John J	m	21-45
KARNES Mary	f	16+	HUTCHENS Sarah	f	16+
PEARSON Levy	m	21-45	HUTCHENS E J	f	16+
PEARSON Marthey J	f	16+	HUTCHENS Wm S	m	10-18
PEARSON Wm G	m	0-10	HUTCHENS Lias G	m	10-18
			HUTCHENS James	m	0-10
			HUCHENS John	m	0-10
[247]			HUTCHENS Ann	f	0-16
PEARSON Emma	f	0-16	HUTCHENS Mary	f	16+
BLOYD William	m	21-45	RAIMY Charity		
BLOYD Deliley	f	16+	RAIMY Wm D	m	10-18
BLOYD John M	m	0-10	RAIMY Annis R	m	10-18
BLOYD Eli	m	0-10	RAINY Henry	m	0-10
JETT Wm A	m	18-21	BLOYD James	m	21-45
HUCHESON William	m	45+	BLOYD Sarah J	f	16+
HUTCHENS John P	m	10-18	BLOYD John F	m	0-10
HUTCHENS Elizabeath	f	16+	BLOYD Mary E	f	0-16
HUTCHENS Sarah A	f	0-16			
HUTCHENS Lias G	m	10-18			
HUTCHENS George W	m	0-10	[251]		
HUTCHENS Manervey C	f	0-16	CHATMAN Wilson	m	45+
HUTCHENS Joseph A	m	0-10	CHATMAN Sarah	f	16+
PERRY Robert	m	45+	CHATMAN Sereaney	f	16+
PERRY Harriet M	f	16+	CARROL Sarah A	f	0-16
PERRY Thomas J	m	10-18	CARROL Mary	f	0-16
PERRY Wm M	m	10-18	CARROL Isaac W	m	0-10
PERRY Richard C	m	0-10	HOPE David	m	21-45
PERRY Benjamin	m	0-10	HOPE Louisa	f	16+
PERRY Marthey E	f	0-16	HOPE Marthey	f	0-16
DYE Richard	m	45+	HOPE James T	m	0-10
DYE Tho H	m	18-21	HOPE Mary E	f	0-16
DYE Julia F	f	0-16	HOPE Sarah A	f	0-16
DYE Calvin M	m	21-45	HOPE Robt H	m	0-10
DYE Charles	m	21-45	MARTIN E A	m	16+
DYE Louisa	f	16+	MARTIN Calep	m	21-45
DYE Sarah J	f	16+	MARTIN Louisa	f	16+
DYE Richard	m	10-18	MARTIN Joseph	m	10-18
			MARTIN Robt	m	10-18
			MARTIN Marthey	f	0-16
[249]			MARTIN James	m	0-10
DYE Harriet	f	0-16	MARTIN Elizabeath	f	0-16
DYE Emma	f	0-16	REED John A	m	45+
NOOT William H	m	45+	REED Sarah	f	16+
NOTT Pheba	f	16+			

REED John	m	18-21	MARSHALL John Wesley	m	10-18
REED James A	m	10-18	MARSHALL B C	f	0-16
REED Sarah J	f	0-16	MARSHALL Mary F	f	0-16
REED George F	m	10-18	MARSHALL Marthey J	f	0-16
REED Nancy A	No entry		MANNON Ira	m	21-45
REED Mary S	f	0-16	MANNON Nancy M	f	16+
REED Jacob	m	0-10	MANNON Hiram H	m	0-10
			MANNON John S	m	0-10
[251]			BULLARD Spencer	m	21-45
BROWN Elizabeath	f	16+	BULLARD Nancy	f	16+
BROWN Margret A	f	0-16	BULLARD Milley	f	0-16
BROWN John W	m	0-10	BULLARD Lidda	f	0-16
BROWN Faancinie	f	0-16	DAVIDSON John	m	21-45
BROWN Henry T	m	0-10	QUINTON Jeffison	m	21-45
BROWN Becy A	f	0-16	QUINTON Cartnir	f	16+
WEEB David	m	21-45	QUINTON Mary C	f	0-16
WEEB Elizabeath	f	16+	QUINTON Alfred R	m	0-10
WEEB John	m	10-18	QUINTON John M	m	0-10
WEEB Josfine	f	0-16	CENTERS Riley	m	21-45
WEEB Sinthey J	f	0-16	CENTERS Sinthey A	f	16+
WEEB Wm	m	0-10			
LITTLE Agus	m	21-45	[257]		
LITTLE Armindey L	f	16+	CENTERS Sarah J	f	0-16
LITTLE Ruthey T	f	0-16	CARTRIGHT Joseph	m	21-45
LITTEL Elizabeath	f	0-16	CARTRIGHT Elizabeath	f	16+
LITTLE John	m	0-10	CARTRIGHT Josephen	f	0-16
LITTEL Samuel	m	0-10	CARTRIGHT Margret	f	0-16
LANE Charles M	m	21-45	CARTRIGHT Samuel	m	0-10
LANE Amanda	f	16+	MANNON Frank	m	21-45
DAVIS Cathern	f	16+	MANNON Leucinda	f	16+
DAVIS Sarah	f	16+	MANNON Hiram	m	0-10
DAVIS Marthey A	f	16+	ANDERSON William	m	21-45
DAVIS Tho J	m	18-21	ANDERSON Marthey	f	16+
DAVIS Nathaniel E	m	10-18	ANDERSON Jas	m	10-18
DAVIS George W	m	21-45	ANDERSON Alfred	m	0-10
TUNE Asbrry	m	21-45	ANDERSON Steaphen	m	0-10
TUNE Nancy A	f	16+	CENTERS Gilfred	m	45+
TUNE James W	m	10-18	CENTERS Laverney	f	16+
TUNN P C	m	10-18	CENTERS Macus	m	18-21
			CENTERS John H	m	0-10
[255]			CENTER Emley J	f	0-16
TUNE Mary	f	0-16	CENTER Sarah E	f	0-16
TUNE Newton J	m	0-10	McKNIGHT Thomas	m	21-45
TUNE Jessee	m	0-10	McKNIGHT Elizabeath	f	16+
TUNE Asberry	m	0-10	McKNIGHT Wm G	m	10-18
SENCYBOY Chritian	m	21-45	McKNIGHT E F	f	0-16
SENCYBOY Elizabeath	f	16+	McKNIGHT John F	m	10-18
SECENBOY A D	m	0-10	McKNIGHT Mary L	f	0-16
MARSHALL C S	m	21-45	McKNIGHT Margret J	f	0-16
MARSHALL Mary E	f	16+	McKNIGHT James W	m	0-10
MARSHALL Jas F	m	10-18	McKNIGHT Tho H	m	0-10

McKNIGHT Marthey L	f	0-16		INGREM Shade	m	21-45
				INGREM Nancy	f	16+
[259]				INGREM A D	m	10-18
TUNE Charles	m	21-45		INGREM John T	m	10-18
TUNE Elizabeath A	f	16+		INGREM Wm M D	m	0-10
TUNE William	m	10-18		INGREM Susan A	f	0-16
TUNE Mary	f	0-16		INGREM Sandy	No entry	
TUNE Shelton	m	10-18		HARRISON Isaac	m	21-45
TUNE Henry	m	0-10		HARRISON Sarah	f	16+
TUNE Aramda	f	0-16		HARRISON Thomas	m	0-10
TUNE James R	m	0-10		HARRISON Patsey	f	0-16
RUTHERFORD Calvin	m	45+		HARRISON John	No entry	
RUTHERFORD Sarah	f	16+				
RUTHERFORD Charltty	f	16+		[263]		
RUTHERFORD Mary B	f	0-16		WEST Hesseykia	m	0-16
RUTHERFORD Winney	f	0-16		BOATRIGHT Elizabeath	f	16+
RUTHERFORD Wm T	m	10-18		FLOID John	m	18-21
RUTHERFORD Balis	m	0-10		HICKS A V	m	45+
RUTHERFORD Robt H	m	0-10		HICKS Malviney	f	16+
RUTHERFORD Sarah E	f	0-16		BASSET John M	m	45+
JOHNSON James	m	45+		BASSET Joseph C	m	10-18
JOHNSON Mary	f	16+		BASSET Mary C	f	0-16
JOHNSON Eliza	f	16+		BASSET Wm S	m	0-10
JOHNSON Telithey	f	0-16		BASSET Isaac H	m	0-10
LEWIS Eliza	m*	45+		YONG Thomas	f*	0-16
LEWIS Nancy	f	16+		YONG Sefroney E	f	16+
LEWIS Wm	m	0-10		YONG Henery	m	10-18
LEWIS	f	0-16		YONG John	m	21-45
LEWIS	f	0-16		YOUNG George W	m	10-18
LEWIS	f	0-16		YONG Leura A	f	0-16
				YONG Tho B	m	0-10
[261]				YOUNG William	m	0-10
WHITE RIVER TOWNSHIP				YOUNG S Nancy E	f	16+
DANNELS R G	m	21-45		YOUNG Samuel M	m	0-10
DANNELS Mary J	f	16+		YOUNG Richard	m	0-10
DANNELS W O	m	0-10		McCINSEY W A	m	45+
DANNELES Susan	f	16+		McCINSEY Mary	f	16+
DANNELS Jeffison	m	18-21		McCINSEY Sarah L	f	0-16
DANNELS Sarah J	f	0-16		HOBS Jessee H	m	45+
DANNELS Elizabeath	f	16+		HOBS Nancy	f	16+
DANNELS Hiley J	f	0-16		HOBS Tho M	m	18-21
DANNELS Sibbey M	f	0-16		HOBS Lewis H	m	10-18
DANNELS Nancy M	f	0-16				
LONG M B	m	45+		[265]		
LONG Lucy	f	16+		HOBS Calebp J	m	0-10
LONG John	m	18-21		HOBS Joseph C	m	0-10
LONG W K	m	18-21		STRICKLER John	m	45+
LONG Nancy A	f	0-16		STRICKLER Liza	f	16+
LONG Theadacia	f	0-16		STRICKLER Mary	f	16+
LONG Mary M	f	0-16		STRICKLER Wm	m	10-18
DUNNUM Henry	m	21-45		STRICKLER Leucinda	f	0-16

STRICKLER Temery	m	10-18	PASCAL Susan F	f	0-16
STRICKLER Narsis	f	0-16	PASCAL S J	f	0-16
STRICKLER	f	0-16	PASCAL Wm W	m	0-10
STRICKLER Rebeca	f	0-16	PASCAL Tho G	m	0-10
STRICKLER Benjamin	m	0-10			
LEWIS Hiram	m	21-45	[269]		
LEWIS Nancy	f	16+	PASCAL Jas A	m	0-10
LEWIS Enous	m	0-10	HARRIS Wm M	m	45+
LEWIS Mary E	f	0-16	HARRIS Stan D	m	21-45
HUTCHENS J W	m	21-45	HARRIS W F	m	18-21
HUTCHENS Mary J	f	16+	HARRIS Wm D M	m	21-45
HUTCHENS Mary	f	0-16	HARRIS B E	f	0-16
HUTCHENS Bales	m	0-10	HARRIS M A	f	0-16
HUTCHENS Sterling	m	0-10	CARRIGEN Mareney	f	16+
HUTCHENS Shelbey	m	0-10	CARRIGEN Wm C	m	10-18
HUTCHENS Ellis	m	45+	CARRIGEN Harret E	f	0-16
HUTCHENS Mary	f	16+	CARRGEN H S	f	0-16
HUTCHENS Alfred	m	10-18	CARRIGEN B C	f	0-16
HUTCHENS White	m	10-18	CARRIGEN Jas P	m	0-10
REED Nathan	m	18-21	CARRGEN John L	m	0-10
REED Nancy	f	16+	CARRGEN Nancy	f	0-16
REED A B	f	10-16	PARKER Pleasant	m	45+
REED J E	m	10-18	PARKER Sarah	f	16+
REED E C	m	0-10	PARKER S B	m	10-18
REED John	m	0-10	PARKER Elizabeath	f	0-16
			PARKER Debby	f	0-16
[267]			PARKER Sarah A	f	0-16
REED Malinda	m*	0-10	PARKER A C	m	0-10
HICKS Eliza	m*	45+	PARKER P R	m	0-10
HICKS A J	m	45+	PARKER P F	m	0-10
HICKS Sarah H	f	16+	MUSTIN J B	m	0-10
HICKS Liza	f	16+	MUSTIN Francis	m	0-16
MANKINS W H	m	21-45	MUSTIN Elizabeath	f	0-16
MANKINS Louisa	f	16+	RUTHERFORD R A	m	45+
PAIN J J	m	45+	RUTHERFORD Mary	f	16+
PAIN E N	f	16+	DOD Sarah	f	16+
PAIN W P	m	18-21	DOD _____	m	18-21
PAIN John W	m	18-21			
PAIN D J	f	16+	[271]		
PAIN Angeline	f	0-16	DOD Robt	m	10-18
PAIN Lucy	f	0-16	DOD Wm	m	0-10
PAIN James J	m	0-10	JONES Margret	f	16+
PAIN Tho S	m	0-10	JONES Nelson	m	10-18
CARRINGEN P M	m	45+	JONES Abslum	m	10-18
CARRIGEN Elizabeeth	f	16+	JONES Robt	m	10-18
FINE Henry	m	21-45	JONES James	m	0-10
FINE Sinthey D	f	16+	JONES Nancy	f	0-16
FINE W J	m	0-10	CARTER B R	m	21-45
FINE	f	0-16	CARTER Lucy C	f	16+
PASCAL Tho	m	21-45	CARTER Tennisee	f	0-16
PASCAL Rachal	f	16+	CARTER Marthy J	f	0-16

CARTER Sarah L	f	0-16		NIKLES Joseph G	m	10-18
CARTER Nancy C	f	0-16		THOMPSON A L	m	21-45
RUNNELS Liza	f	16+		THOMPSON Sarah J	f	16+
RUNNELS Elizabeath	f	16+		THOMPSON Henry L	m	0-10
RUNNELS George	m	10-18		THOMPSON W G	m	0-10
RUNNELS Carline	f	0-16		THOMPSON J S	m	0-10
HARRIS Samuel	m	18-21		HANNA Jerrymire	m	45+
HARRIS Mary W	f	16+		HANNA Mary A	f	16+
HARRIS Wm H	m	0-10		HANNA Mary A	f	16+
HUNT William	m	45+		HANNA Jerrymire C	m	18-21
HUNT Julia	f	16+		HANNA Rebeca J	f	0-16
RAIMMY Meda	f	16+		HANNA Margret	f	0-16
PORTER William	m	21-45		HANNA Pet	m	0-10
PORTER Sarah E	f	16+		HANNA James	m	21-45
PORTER Zachary T	m	18-21		HANNA Harriet	f	16+
PORTER G J	No entry			HANNA Samul	m	21-45
				HANNA Flemmon E	f	16+
				HANNA Flemmon E	m	0-10
[273]				HANNA Huston	f	0-16
PORTER Mary	f	16+		HANNA Flennon	f	0-16
PORTER William	m	10-18		HUSE John	m	21-45
PORTER Aaron	m	0-10		HUSE Susanna	f	16+
PORTER Mithell	m	0-10		UUSE Sarah J	f	0-16
PORTER Sarah E	f	16+		HUSE Jerrymire	m	0-10
EASON Luther	m	21-45		RAMSEY Joel	m	21-45
EASON Mary A	f	16+		RAMSEY Mary E	f	16+
EASON Sarah R	f	0-16		RAMSEY Mary	f	0-16
THARP Jessie	m	45+		BROOKS Lafayete	m	21-45
THARP L R	f	16+		BROOKS J T	f	16+
THARP E M	f	16+		BROOKS Wm T	m	10-18
THARP John L	m	18-21				
THARP N A	f	0-16		[277]		
THARP Pesselley	f	0-16		BROOKS Sarah F	f	0-16
THARP Mary E	f	0-16		BROOKS James M	m	10-18
THARP Rachal	f	0-16		BROOKS Mary A	f	0-16
THARP George W	m	0-10		BROOKS John W	m	0-10
THARP Susan J	f	0-16		BROOKS Louisa J	f	0-16
THARP Jas L	m	0-10		LEWIS George	m	45+
LEWIS M B	m	45+		LEWIS Rebeca	f	16+
LEWIS Narsis J	f	16+		LEWIS Danniel K	m	18-21
LEWIS James A	m	10-18		LEWIS James K	m	18-21
LEWIS N P	m	0-10		LEWIS Amanda J	f	16+
LEWIS B F	m	0-10		LEWIS Mary	f	0-16
LEWIS Jacob M	m	0-10		LEWIS Ruthey	f	0-16
LEWIS George W	m	21-45		LEWIS Marthey	f	0-16
LEWIS Letty	f	16+		LEWIS George	m	0-10
LEWIS Sarah	f	16+		LEWIS Rebeca	f	0-16
LEWIS Leviney	f	0-16		LEWIS Callafornia	f	0-16
				STOUT Johnithan	m	45+
[275]				STOUT Margret	f	16+
LEWIS Matilda	f	0-16		STOUT David S	m	18-21
REAH Frances	m	0-10		STOUT Jerymire	m	10-18

STOUT William	m	18-21
STOUT James	m	10-18
STOUT Sinthey	f	16+
STOUT Julia A	f	16+
STOUT Kizzia J	f	16+
STOUT Samuel J	m	18-21
STOUT Marthey	f	16+
STOUT Robt C	m	0-10
VANHOOSE John J	m	45+
VANHOOSE Rachal	f	16+
VANHOOSE Charity	f	16+
[279]		
VANHOOSE Mary A	f	16+
VANHOOSE Lida J	f	16+
VANHOOSE Leucinda	f	0-16
VANHOOSE George W	m	10-18
VANHOOSE Elizabeath	f	0-16
VANHOOSE Zacrier	m	0-10
VANHOOSE John	m	0-10
VANHOOSE Jacob M	m	0-10
VANHOOSE Annis A	f	0-16
LEWIS Bracken	m	45+
LEWIS Emiline	f	16+
LEWIS Malida	f	0-16
LEWIS James W	m	10-18
LEWIS Albert C	m	0-10
LEWIS Tho B	m	0-10
LEWIS Matilda	f	0-16
DICKISON Rachal	f	16+
DICKISON Annetty	f	16+
DICKISON Robt	m	18-21
DICKISON Louesey	f	16+
DICKISON Mary E	f	0-16
DICKISON Albert P	m	10-18
DICKSON John G	m	0-10
BURRIS J C	m	21-45
BURRIS Marthey J	f	16+
BURRIS Taylor	m	18-21
BURRIS James	m	10-18
BURRIS Elizabeath	f	0-16
BURRIS _allin	m	0-10
BURRIS Sarah	f	16+
[281]		
CAMBPLE Julia	f	16+
CAMBPLE James B	m	18-21
CAMBPLE William	m	10-18
CAMBPLEE Joseph W	m	10-18
CAMBPLE Mary E	f	0-16
CAMBPLEE Thomas	m	0-10

CAMBPLEE Noel	m	0-10
CAMBPLEE Richard	m	0-10
ROBBINSON John	m	45+
ROBBINSON Percilley	f	16+
ROBINSON Liza R	f	16+
ROBBINSON Annis A	f	0-16
ROBBINSON Tho H	m	21-45
ROBBINSON Emiline	f	16+
ROBBINSON Sharlote J	f	0-16
ROBBNSON Henry M	m	0-10
ROBBINSON Robt N	m	0-10
ROBBINSON Mary B	f	0-16
ROBBINSON Harret	f	0-16
JONES James A	m	18-21
JONES Leviney	f	16+
JONES Emiline	f	0-16
JONES Susan E	f	0-16
JONES William A	m	10-18
JONES Rachal M	f	0-16
JONES Rebeca J	f	0-16
JONES James M	m	0-10
JONES Thomas B	m	0-10
[283]		
CONLEY B C	m	21-45
CONLEY Annaliza	f	16+
CONLEY Serildey	f	0-16
CONLEY William M	m	10-18
CONLEY Julia	f	0-16
CONLEY Mason S	m	0-10
CONLEY Henry J	m	0-10
CONLEY James B	m	0-10
BALLARD William	m	21-45
BALLARD Rachal	f	16+
BALLARD Nancy J	f	0-16
BALLARD Mary T	f	0-16
BALLARD Peter	m	0-10
BALLARD William H	m	0-10
BALLARD George	m	0-10
BALLARD Narsis	f	0-16
MILLS Eda	f	16+
MILLS Franklin	m	18-21
MILLS Sarah E	f	16+
MILLS E P	m	10-18
MILLS Tolbert	m	0-10
MILLS Netty E	f	0-16
MILLS Mary B	f	0-16
MILLS Sith L	m	0-10
MILLS Jacob	m	0-10
WINKLER Henry	m	21-45
WINKLER William H	m	18-21

WINKLER Lear	f	16+
WINKLER Lear Gemimey	f	0-16
[285]		
WINKLER John R	m	10-18
WINKLER Samuel	m	0-10
WINKLER George	m	0-10
WINKLER Robbert	m	0-10
WINKLER Nancy A	f	16+
JONES Riley	m	45+
JONES Nancy	f	16+
JONES Elizabeath	f	16+
JONES Emiline	f	16+
JONES Neal	m	10-18
JONES Jessee	m	18-21
JONES John	m	10-18
JONES David	m	10-18
JONES William	m	0-10
JONES Benjamin	m	0-10
DICKISON James	m	45+
DICKISON Milley	f	16+
DICKISON Semanthey	f	0-16
DICKISON James	m	10-18
DICKISON Umphrey	m	0-10
DICKISON Rufus B	m	0-10
CARTER George W	m	45+
CARTER Nancy	f	16+
CARTER Charls P	m	18-21
CARTER Jordon H	m	18-21
CARTER George W	m	10-18
BUCHANAN Catherine	f	16+
McCRISTINAN David H	m	10-18
FLOID Marthey	f	0-16
[287]		
CARTER Lewis B	m	21-45
CARTER Roda E	f	16+
LONG Mary	f	16+
LONG Matilda J	f	0-16
LONG Thomas	m	10-18
LONG Bisey	f	0-16
LONG Elisha	m	0-10
ARAMOORE Joseph	m	21-45
ARAMOORE Mary J	f	16+
ARAMOORE James J	m	10-18
ARRAMORE Liza J	f	0-16
ARRAMORE J R	m	10-18
ARAMORE Jacob P	m	0-10
ARAMOORE Susan A	f	0-16
ARAMORE Margret J		No entry
ARAMOORE Abrem C	m	0-10

COLCLEASURE Margret J	f	16+
COLCLEASURE Liza A	f	16+
B_____ John S	m	18-21
WILLIAMS Oliver	m	21-45
WILLIAMS Jane	f	16+
WILLIAMS Mary E	f	16+
WILLIAMS Jas W	m	18-21
WILLIAMS Sarah M	f	16+
WILLIAMS Isaac H	m	10-18
WILLIAMS John R	m	10-18
WILLIAMS L A	m	0-10
WILLIAMS Hanna J	f	0-16
WILLIAMS Mannervy J	f	0-16
WILLIAMS Leucinda M	f	0-16
[289]		
WILLIAMS Telithey T	f	0-16
LEE James	m	18-21
LEE Susan A	f	16+
LEE Sarah E	f	0-16
BRADSHAW Charls	m	18-21
BRADSHAW Temperence	f	16+
BRADSHAW Henry A	m	0-10
BRADSHAW John T	m	0-10
MASON D C	m	21-45
MASON Francis J	f	16+
MASON Zacrier C	m	0-10
MASON John C	m	0-10
MASON James H	m	0-10
WEST Rachal	f	16+
WEST John L	m	21-45
WEST Marthey J	f	16+
WEST James S	m	18-21
WEST William	m	0-10
CARTER John C	m	18-21
CARTER Hailey M	f	16+
MAYS James L	m	21-45
MAYS Lidda J	f	16+
HANNA Sarah	f	16+
HANNA Peter	m	18-21
EVANS James	m	18-21
HANNA George	m	10-18
HANNA Marthey	f	0-16
STRAIN Robt	m	21-45
STRAIN Perciler	f	16+
[291]		
VANHOOSE John	m	45+
VANHOOSE Mary	f	16+
MANKINS Peter	m	18-21
MANKINS Bashaba	f	16+

MANKINS Carrol	m	0-10	HARRIS Theadore	m	0-10	
MANKINS Malind	f	0-16	HARRIS Mary B	f	0-16	
HELBERT Sarah	f	16+	HARRIS Jeffison	m	0-10	
HEBBERT Henry C	m	18-21	HARRIS H L	m	45+	
HEBBERT James M	m	18-21	STEWARD Tho	m	18-21	
HELBERT Porter	m	10-18	STWED Nancy A	f	16+	
HELBERT Marthey N	f	0-16				
HELBERT George	m	10-18	[295]			
HELBERT Sarah S	f	0-16	STEWARD Alley J	f	0-16	
HELBERT William L D	m	0-10	STEWARD Mandaney P	f	0-16	
MILLS Margret	f	16+	STEUARD Sarah T	f	0-16	
MILLS Susan C	f	0-16	STEWARD Marthey E	f	0-16	
MILLS Leviney E	f	0-16	PASCAL John	No entry		
MILLS Sarah J	f	0-16	PASCAL Rachal	f	16+	
MILLS Amanda E	f	0-16	PASCAL Alfred	m	10-18	
HENSON Jessee	m	18-21	PASCAL Jas M	m	10-18	
HENSON William	m	45+	PASCAL Jessee	m	0-10	
HENSON Leviney	f	16+	PASCAL John	m	0-10	
MULINIX T J	m	18-21	PASCAL Mort A	m	0-10	
MULINX Elizabeath	f	16+	PASCAL Sarah E	f	0-16	
THOMPSON Mary H	f	16+	STINNETT A J	m	21-45	
THOMPSON J C	m	18-21	STINNET Malinda	f	16+	
THOMPSON Mary	f	16+	STINNET Amanda J	f	0-16	
RAIMY Owen	m	45+	STINNET Sarah A	f	0-16	
RAIMY Benjamin	m	18-21	STINNET William	m	0-10	
RAIMY Barbey E	f	16+	STINNET John	m	0-10	
			STINNET James	m	0-10	
[293]			HOPPERS Micle	m	21-45	
RAIMY Efriem	m	18-21	HOPPER Nancy	f	16+	
RAIMY William B	m	10-18	HOPPER William F	m	0-10	
RAIMY Sarah E	f	0-16	HOPPER George M	m	0-10	
RAIMY Albert	m	10-18	HOPPER John H	m	0-10	
RAIMY Nancy A	f	0-16	HOPPER Jasper	m	0-10	
RAIMY Margret	f	0-16	HOPPER E C	f	0-16	
RAIMY Henry	m	0-10	CARRIGEN James M	m	21-45	
RAIMY Elizabeath	f	16+	CARRGEN Marthey	f	16+	
SPRIGSTON Wm	m	45+	CARRIGEN Mary	f	16+	
SPRIGSTON Emiline	f	16+	CARRIGEN John	m	18-21	
SPRIGSTON Williamson	m	21-45	CARRGEN Annie	f	0-16	
SPRIGSTON Warren	f*	16+				
SPRIGSTON Melviney	f	16+	[297]			
SPRIGSTON Steaphen	m	0-10	CARRGEN Jane	f	0-16	
SPRIGSTON Ellen	f	0-16	CARRGEN Pallistin	f	0-16	
SPRIGSTON R J	f	0-16	CARRGEN Harriet	f	0-16	
SPRIGSTON James	m	0-10	CARRIGEN James	m	0-10	
SPRIGSTON Mary	f	0-16	LEWIS Bracen	m	45+	
HARRIS Issabella	f	16+	LEWIS Zacrier	m	18-21	
HARRIS Robt	m	18-21	LEWIS Matilda	f	16+	
HARRIS James	m	18-21	LEWIS John	m	18-21	
HARRIS Alx	m	10-18	LEWIS Eliferous	m	18-21	
HARRIS F M	m	0-10	McCINSEY John	m	45+	

1865 SHERIFF'S CENSUS OF WASHINGTON COUNTY ARKANSAS

McCINSEY Jane	f	16+	[301]		
McCINSEY Ailsey	f	16+	HARRIS William M	m	10-18
McCINSEY Wm	m	18-21	HARRIS Thomas C	m	10-18
McCINSEY Zacrier	f	10-18	HARRIS B F	m	0-10
McCINSEY Margret	f	0-16	HARRIS E G	m	0-10
McCINSEY Deliley	f	0-16	MANKINS Peter	m	45+
McCINSEY Heny	m	0-10	MANKINS Easter	f	16+
McCINSEY John	m	45+	MANKINS Walter	m	18-21
BOYD John	m	45+	GILBAND Clementine	f	0-16
BOYD Mary	f	16+	MANKINS Elizabeath	f	0-16
BOYD James A	m	18-21	MANKINS Sarah	f	0-16
BOYD John W	m	0-10	MANKINS Peter	m	0-10
BOYD Mary B	f	0-16	MANKINS Peter Snr	m	45+
HEUGS Sarah	No entry		HANNA James	m	45+
HEUGS Thomas	m	18-21	HANNA Mary	f	16+
HEUGS Daniel	m	18-21	HANNA Phil	m	FPC
HUGS Samuel	m	10-18	HANNA Nig	m	FPC
HEUGS Marthy	f	0-16	MANKINS Ellen	f	FPC
HUGS Joseph	m	21-45			
HEUGS Liza	f	16+	RICHLAND TOWNSHIP		
			SMITH Mary J	f	+16
			SMITH Mary E	f	+16
[299]			SMITH Rebeca A	f	0-16
LEE Marien	m	18-21	SMITH Sarah	f	0-16
LEE Jane	f	16+	SMITH Thomas	m	10-18
LEE Gracy A	f	16+	SMITH Cate	f	0-16
LEE John	m	21-45	SMITH Allice	f	0-16
LEE Margret	f	0-16	SMITH Lee H	m	0-10
LEE Eliza	m*	0-10	VINZANT Sarah	f	+16
LEE Rasan	f	0-16			
BOYD William A	m	21-45			
BOYD Rebeca A	f	16+	[303]		
BOYD Susan	f	0-16	HARRIS Mary	f	+16
LEWIS Elizabeath	f	16+	HARRIS G W	m	10-18
LEWIS Mary J	f	16+	SHERROD William	m	+45
LEWIS Mathew	m	18-21	SHERROD Charlote	f	+16
LEWIS Nathan	m	10-18	WILLIAMS Mosses	m	18-21
LEWIS Brackin	m	10-18	WILLIAMS Charlote	f	+16
LEWIS Eda	f	0-16	WILLIAMS Garret	m	18-21
LEWIS Sarah	f	0-16	WILLIAMS Nancy	f	+16
LEWIS Henry	m	0-10	WILLIAMS William R	m	10-18
MILLER Pleasant	m	21-45	WILLIAMS Mary	f	0-16
MILLER Margret	f	16+	WILLIAMS Tho J	m	0-10
RAMSEY William Harris	m	18-21	WILLIAMS Matilda J	f	0-16
RAMSEY Sarah	f	16+	WILLIAMS John W	m	0-10
RAMSEY Ellender	f	0-16	WILLIAMS Sterling P	m	0-10
RAMSEY John	m	0-10	DENTON Jacob	m	45+
HARRIS J B	m	21-45	DENTON Lidda	f	16+
HARRIS Sarah A	f	16+	DENTON William	m	10-18
HARRIS Julias N	m	18-21	ALLRED Gamblen	m	21-45
HARRIS Samuel A	m	10-18	ALLRED Mary	f	+16
HARRIS John W	m	10-18	ALLRED John D	m	0-10

Name	Sex	Age
ALLRED Louisa J	f	0-16
ALLRED Sarah E	f	0-16
WEEB Joel H	m	21-45
WEEB Margret E	f	16+
WEEB P E	f	0-16
WEEB Wm A	m	10-18
WEEB James H	m	10-18
WEEB John P	m	0-10
WEEB Perry T	m	0-10
[305]		
WEEB Annaliza	f	0-16
WEEB Ellenora C	f	0-16
WILLIAMS R R	m	45+
WILLIMAS Catherine	f	16+
WILLIAMES James	m	10-18
WILLIAMS David	m	10-18
WILLIAMS Andrew	m	10-18
WILLILAMS Narsis	f	0-16
WILLIAMS Florrance	f	0-16
WILLIAMS John	m	21-45
WILLIAMS Marthey C	f	16+
WILLIAMS A L	m	0-10
WILLIAMS Mary T	f	0-16
WILLIAMS Joseph	m	21-45
WILLIAMS Samuel	m	18-21
WILLIAMES Julia A	f	16+
KESTERS H W	m	21-45
KESTERS Sharlote	f	16+
KESTERS Nancy J	f	16+
KESTERS James J	m	0-10
KESTERS Fancis A	m	0-10
KESTERS George M	m	0-10
WILLIAMS Lewis	m	45+
LEWIS Mary	f	16+
LEWIS Jas J	m	18-21
LEWIS Harriet M	f	16+
LEWIS Sarah	f	0-16
LEWIS John A	m	0-10
LEWIS Nancy	f	0-16
[307]		
LEWIS Marthey T	f	0-16
RAGER Marthey J	f	16+
RAGER Sarah	f	0-16
RAGER Lafayete	m	10-18
RAGER Tennisee S	f	0-16
FROST T W	m	21-45
FROST Mary	f	16+
FROST W D	m	18-21
FROST John L	m	10-18
FROST Sarah C	f	0-16
FROST Benjamin	m	10-18
FROST Edward D	m	10-18
FROST Tho E	m	0-10
FROST Joseph	m	0-10
FROST Mary M	f	0-16
BUCHANAN Robbert	m	45+
BUCHANAN Mary	f	16+
KING William	m	10-18
CUNNINGHAM Florene	m	0-10
CUNNINGHAM Willey	f	0-16
HENDERSON Wm B	m	45+
HENDERSON Sarah	f	16+
HENDERSON William	m	18-21
HENDERSON Isaac	m	10-18
HENDERSON Margret	f	16+
HENDERSON Marthey	f	16+
SMITH Martin	m	21-45
SMITH Liza	f	0-16
SMITH Summerfield	m	10-18
[308]		
SMITH Luviney	f	0-16
SMITH Franklin	m	0-10
SMITH Elizabeath	f	0-16
WILLIAMS Warren	m	21-45
MASTERS John	m	21-45
MASTERS Ann	f	16+
MASTERS David J	m	18-21
MASTERS Mary F	f	16+
MASTERS Marthey J	f	0-16
MASTERS Nancy A	f	0-16
MASTERS Sarah A	f	0-16
MASTERS Narsis J	f	0-16
MASTERS Arrazana	f	0-16
MASTERS John L	m	0-10
MASTERS William P	m	0-10
SMITH D T	m	21-45
SMITH E J	f	16+
SMITH J M	m	21-45
SMITH J A	m	21-45
SMITH R J	f	16+
SMITH George W	m	10-18
SMITH P F	m	10-18
SMITH Danniel F	m	10-18
SMITH Sarah E	f	0-16
SMITH Berana T	f	0-16
SMITH Jeffison D	m	0-10
SMITH Louesey	f	0-16
WILLIFORD Washington	m	21-45
WILLIFORD Eliz	f	16+

WILLIFORD Mary H	f	0-16	FOSTER Mary		f	0-16
WILLIFORD Lucy J	f	0-16	FOSTER Cassander		f	0-16
			FOSTER Aaron		m	0-10
[310]			FOSTER Sarah		f	0-16
WILLIFORD Tho J	m	0-10	FOSTER David		m	0-10
WILLIFORD A C	m	45+	FOSTER Richard		m	0-10
BENBROOK Ewing	m	45+	FOSTER George		m	0-10
BENBROOK Mahaley	f	16+	WILLIAMS Tho W		m	21-45
BENBROOK Hosey M	m	18-21	WILLIAMS Sarah E		f	0-16
BENBROOK Nancy J	f	16+	WILLIAMS Francis J		f	0-16
BENBROOK Jarret T	m	10-18	WILLIAMS E E		m	0-10
BENBROOK Harriet E	f	0-16	WILLIAMS Mell R		f	0-16
BENBROOK Charles M	m	10-18	McGARRAH Mathew		m	21-45
BENBROOK John H	m	0-10	McGARRAH Jas S		m	21-45
BENBROOK L C	f	0-16				
BENBROOK E C	f	0-16	[314]			
BENBROOK Smith L	m	0-10	COLDWELL Jas A		m	10-18
BENBROOK Rebeca	f	16+	COLDWELL J W		m	10-18
RITTER Young	m	45+	COLDWELL Sinthy A		f	0-16
RITTER Malvina	f	16+	COLDWELL Wm L		m	0-10
RITTER Marthey J	f	16+	COLDWELL Mary E		f	0-16
RITTER Mary	f	16+	COLDWELL Samuel C		m	0-10
RITTER A J	m	18-21	COLDWELL Nancy A		f	0-16
RITTER Mahaley	f	16+	COLDWELL J R		m	0-10
RITTER Ellen	f	0-16	COLDWELL Francis G		No	entry
HASH A C	m	21-45	DYAR Jackson		m	45+
HASH Bellzona M	f	0-16	DYAR Agnes		f	16+
HASH James L	m	0-10	DYAR Nancy A		f	16+
HASH Wm A	m	0-10	DYAR Sinthey A		f	16+
HASH Ester	f	0-16	DYAR Wm V		m	18-21
HASH B F	m	21-45	DYAR C B		m	10-18
COLDWELL William	m	21-45	DYAR Mary A		f	0-16
COLDWELL Mary H	f	16+	DYAR C C		m	0-10
COLDWELL A M	m	10-18	STOKENBERRY Harmon		m	21-45
			STOKENBERRY Jane		f	16+
[312]			STOKENBERRY Henry		m	10-18
BERA Samuel	m	21-45	STOKENBERRY R		m	0-10
BERA Marthey A	f	16+	STOKENBERRY Sarah		f	0-16
CARNAN Isaac	m	45+	KYRKLAND T E		f	16+
CARNAN Permelia	f	16+	KYRKLAND Maxim		m	10-18
CARNAN Isaac	m	21-45	VAUGHN Wm		m	18-21
CARMAN Edda	m	21-45	DRAIN George W		m	45+
CARMAN Tho J	m	21-45	DRAIN Elizabeath		f	16+
WILLIAMS A J	m	21-45	DRAIN Richard		m	18-21
WILLIAMS Carline	f	16+	DRAIN James H		m	10-18
WILLIAMS Nathaniel	m	0-10	DRAIN Leutica		f	0-16
WILLIAMS Colley	m	0-10				
WILLIAMS Cornela	No	entry	[316]			
FOSTER John	m	21-45	CATE Charls		m	21-45
FOSTER Nancy	f	16+	CATE Martha		f	16+
FOSTER Wm	m	10-18	CATE John		m	21-45

CATE Mary	f	0-16	HOOD David L	m	0-10	
CATE Willice	m	0-10	SANDERS H N	m	18-21	
KELLEY T J	f	0-16	SANDERS Roda	f	16+	
KELLEY Elizabeath	f	16+	SANDERS George E	m	0-10	
KELLEY William T	m	10-18	SANDERS Jackson	m	0-10	
KELLEY Margaret A	f	16+	SANDERS Caldona	f	0-16	
KELLEY Medlene	f	16+	MAGUIRE Danniel	m	18-21	
KELLEY John H	m	0-10	MAGUIRE Mary	f	16+	
MILLER S J	m	45+	MGURER Nancy	f	0-16	
MILLER Thomas	f*	0-16	MAGUIRE Mary	f	0-16	
MILLER Caly	f	16+	MAGAUIRE Sarah	f	0-16	
MILLER Maryan	f	16+				
MILLER Elizabeath	f	16+	[320]			
HOWLL Ramey	m	0-10	STEVEN Maryan	f	0-16	
WARD William	m	10-18	STEVENS _aack	m	0-10	
BUCKHANAN A	m	FPC	STEVENS Nancy	f	0-16	
VAUGHN Charley	m	FPC	STEVENS Matildia	f	0-16	
VAUGHN Maneta	f	FPC	STEVENS Henry	m	0-10	
VAUGHN Dave	m	FPC	STEVENS Stone	m	0-10	
VAUGHN Dervy	m	FPC	WILLIAM David T	f*	0-16	
HELTON Volinelind	f	16+	WILLIAM Matildia	f	16+	
HELTON E C	f	16+	WILLIAMS Mandrenah	f	16+	
WALUP Finley	m	45+	WILLIAM Mary Jane	f	16+	
WALKUP Haner	f	16+	OSBURN Johnathan	m	21-45	
WALKUP Mary	f	0-16	OZBURN Marthy A	f	16+	
WALKUP Analiza	f	0-16	OZBURN Levina	f	0-16	
WALKUP Samuel	m	10-18	OZBURN Lucindia	f	0-16	
WALKUP E C	f	0-16	OZBURN Henry	m	10-18	
WALKUP Rosan	f	0-16	OZBURN Maryann	f	0-16	
WALKUP Haner Jan	f	0-16	OZBURN Lydia	f	0-16	
			OZBURN Elen	f	0-16	
[318]			[322]			
DRAIN William	m	0-10				
DRAIN Nancy	m*	45+	WRITE B C	m	45+	
DRAIN Wesley	m	0-10	WRIGHT Ann	f	16+	
DRAIN Vianney	f	0-16	WRIGHT Jas S	m	18-21	
DRAIN Peliney	f	0-16	WRIGHT George W	m	18-21	
CLARK Amburs	m	45+	WRIGHT John H	m	10-18	
CLARK Seliney	f	16+	WRIGHT Mary A	f	0-16	
CLARK Mary	f	16+	WRIGHT Wm T	m	0-10	
CLARK Francis	f	16+	WRIGHT Angeline	f	0-16	
CLARK Marthey E	f	16+	WRIGHT Jacob W	m	0-10	
CLARK Easter	f	16+	WRIGHT Oziney	m	0-10	
CLARK William	m	10-18	REED Robt W	m	21-45	
CLARK John	m	10-18	REED Mary J	f	16+	
CLARK Medlene	f	0-16	BOON Susan A	f	16+	
CLARK Josefen	f	0-16	BOON Turun	m	10-18	
CLARK Ida E	f	0-16	BOON Pernolia	f	0-16	
CLARK Lidda	f	0-16	BOON Inus	f	0-16	
HOOD Jas F	m	18-21	BOON Edward	m	0-10	
HOOD Rebeca	f	16+	SHUMATE Balis	m	45+	

1865 SHERIFF'S CENSUS OF WASHINGTON COUNTY ARKANSAS

WILLIFORD James	m	21-45
WILLIFORD Elizabeath	f	16+
WILLIFORD Mary	f	16+
WILLIFORD Nancy M	m	0-16
WILLIFORD William	m	10-18
WILLIFORD George	m	10-18
WILLIFORD Charles	m	0-10
WILLIFORD Harret	f	0-16
SHUMATE William	m	21-45
SHUMATE Sarah	f	16+
SUMATE Balis	m	0-10
SUNATE Benjman	m	21-45

[325]

SHUMATE Claracy	f	16+
SUMATE Nancy	f	0-16
SHUMATE Mark	m	10-18
TAWLER T A	m	21-45
TAWLER Mary E	f	16+
TAWLER Margrette	f	16+
TAWLER James	m	10-18
TAWLER Nanney	f	0-16
TAWLER John	m	0-10
TAWLER Mary M	f	0-16
GOODRAGE Margret	f	16+
GOODRAGE Francis	f	0-16
GOODRAGE Lonra	f	0-16
GOODRGE Allice	f	0-16
GOODRGE Ester	f	0-16
STRAIN George	m	45+
STRAIN Mary	f	16+
STRAIN Benjamin	m	18-21
STRAIN Jane	f	16+
STRAIN George	m	10-18
STRAIN Andrew	m	10-18
STRAIN James	m	0-10
WOOD Henry	m	21-45
WOOD Catherne	f	16+
WOOD Harvy	m	18-21
WOOD Smith	m	10-18
WOOD Thomas	m	0-10
MOLDEN Jane	f	16+
MOLDEN William P	m	10-18
MOLDEN Jane	f	0-16
MOLDEN Verginia	f	0-16

[328]

MOLDEN Sarah	f	0-16
FINCHER John	m	21-45
FINCHER Indiannia	f	16+
FINCHER Sarah C	f	0-16
FINCHER Harret T	f	0-16
FINCHER H A	m	0-10
CLARK Norris	m	21-45
CLARK Leucinda	f	16+
CLARK Richard	m	18-21
CLARK Ellerry N	m	10-18
WILLIAMS D W	m	45+
WILLIAMS Mary	f	16+
WILLIAMS Sarah	f	16+
WILLIAMS Evinline	f	0-16
THOMPSON A J	m	45+
THOMPSON Pheba	f	16+
THOMPSON Henry	m	18-21
THOMPSON Lucresey	f	16+
THOMPSON Lewis	m	18-21
THOMPSON Mary	f	0-16
CARTER John	m	45+
CARTER Elizabeath	f	16+
CARTER Percilley	f	16+
CARTER Naoma	f	16+
HUNT T J	m	18-21
HUNT Matilda E	f	16+
HUNT Ellenora M	f	0-16
HUNT V J	f	0-16
WILLIAMS John	m	45+
WILLIAMS Hanna	f	16+
WILLIAMS Wilson	f	21-45

[330]

WILLIAMS Mary	f	0-16
WILLIAMS Charity	f	0-16
WILLIAMS Elizabeath	f	0-16
WILLIAMS Hugh R	m	18-21
BROWN Tho R	m	45+
BROWN Nancy C	f	16+
BROWN Mary	f	16+
BROWN William	m	10-18
BROWN C A	f	0-16
BROWN Tho	m	10-18
BROWN Jackson	m	0-10
MALOY Tho	m	18-21
MALOY D M	m	0-10
WHITE John S	m	18-21
WHITE Mary A	f	16+
WHITE Dolly A	f	0-16
WHITE Appy J	f	0-16
WHITE Wm	m	0-10
WHITE Sarah	m*	45+
WHITE Mary	m*	45+
COOPPER Allen	m	18-21
COOPPER Catherrine	f	16+

49

1865 SHERIFF'S CENSUS OF WASHINGTON COUNTY ARKANSAS

COOPPER H R	m	0-10	TRAMMEL G S	m	21-45
COOPPER D J	f	0-16	TRAMMEL Mary E	f	16+
COOPPER Leucinda	f	0-16	TRAMMEL N S	m	10-18
COOPPER Nancy A	f	0-16	TRAMMEL Ann E	f	0-16
WAITS Bethal	m	21-45	TRAMMEL E C	m	0-10
WAITS Nancy	f	16+	TRAMMEL G E	m	0-10
WAITS Allen	m	18-21	SMITH Thomas	m	45+
WAITS Emiline	f	16+	RUNNELS Jas A	m	21-45
WAITS John	m	10-18	RUNNELS Mary E	f	16+
			RUNNELS Benn A	m	0-10
[332]			WADKINS Isac	m	21-45
WAITS Joseph	m	0-10	WADKINS Mary	f	16+
WAITS Washington	m	0-10	WADKINS Enous	m	10-18
WAITS Henry	m	0-10	WADKINS Leucinda	f	0-16
SHEALDS R S	m	21-45	WADKINS Elizabeath	f	0-16
SHEALDS Louisa	f	0-16	WADKINS David	m	0-10
SHEALDS Sarah	m	0-16	WADKINS Ellender	f	0-16
SHEALDS A M	m	18-21	WADKINS Mary	f	0-16
SHEALDS Robt C	m	10-18	WADKINS Isaac	m	0-10
COLDWELL James	m	21-45	WILLIAMS Rile	m	45+
COLDWELL Nancy	f	16+	WILLIAMS Cetty	f	16+
COLDWELL James	m	18-21	WILLIAMS Warren	m	21-45
COLDWELL Jasper	m	10-18	HENDERSON D A	f	16+
COLDWELL Lafayete	m	10-18	WILLIAMS Matilda A	No	entry
COLDWELL D W	m	10-18	PHILLIPPS Kitty	f	16+
MITCHEL William	m	18-21			
MITCHEL Elizabeath	f	16+	[336]		
MITCHEL Richard	m	0-10	HENDERSON Dallis	f	16+
MITCHEL Lenord	m	0-10	HENDERSON Sarah J	f	16+
MITCHEL Jeffison	m	0-10	WILLIAMS E T	m	18-21
SHARP Sofier	f	16+	BANKS J L	m	10-18
SHARP Levy B	m	10-18	WILLIAMS B S	m	10-18
SHARP Milley J	m*	45+	MAGAUIRE G B	m	45+
SHARP John A	m	10-18	MAGAUIRE Nancy A	f	16+
SHARP Fletcher	m	10-18	MAGAUIRE George W	m	10-18
SHARP L E	m	45+	MAGAUIRE A A	m	10-18
SHARP Carline	m*	45+	MAGAUIRE H J	m	10-18
SHARP James	m	0-10	MAGAUIRE J M	m	0-10
BRUNK Joseph	m	21-45	MAGAUIRE W M	m	0-10
BRUNK Carline	f	16+	MAGAUIRE Eliza E	f	0-16
BRUNK Emiline	m*	45+	MAGAUIRE Nancy M	f	0-16
BRUK Joseph B	m	0-10	MAGAUIRE Eliza	f	16+
			BEARD Nancy	f	16+
[334]			BEARD Willie	m	0-10
MITCHEL Richard	m	45+	BEARD Eliza	f	0-16
MITCHEL Sinthey	f	16+	WEST Mary M	f	0-16
MITCHEL Marthy A	f	16+	TRAMMEL Garnet	m	45+
MITCHEL John	m	10-18	PIPER William	m	10-18
MITCHEL Carline	f	0-16	TRAMMEL Pats	m	FPC
MITCHEL Nancy	f	0-16	TRAMMEL James	f*	FPC
MITCHEL Harret	f	0-16	TRAMMEL Milley	f	FPC

TRAMMEL Peter	f*	FPC	GREATHOUSE N G	m	0-10
TRAMMEL George	m	10-18	GREATHOUSE B B	m	0-10
TRAMMEL George	m	10-18	MAYS William	m	21-45
TRAMMEL L P	m	21-45	MAYS Louiza	No	entry
TRAMMEL Nancy J	f	16+	MAYS Samuel	m	10-18
TRAMMEL C F	No	entry	MAYS Robt	m	10-18
TRAMMEL A J	m	18-21	MAYS Albert	m	0-10
			MAYS Jas	m	0-10
[338]			MAYS Tho	m	0-10
TRAMMEL Mary H	f	16+	MAYS L J	f	0-16
TRAMMEL J P	m	10-18	JOHNSONS S E	m	10-18
TRAMMEL Sarah L	f	0-16	JOHNSON S A	m	10-18
TRAMMEL Henry	m	0-10	JOHNSON A J	m	18-21
TRAMMEL Robt W	m	0-10	JOHNSON Matilda	m*	10-18
TRAMMEL L J	f	0-16	JOHNSON Mary E	f	16+
TRAMMEL Tho	m	0-10	JOHNSON Ellen	f	16+
TRAMMEL R A	f	0-16	HOLT T P	No	entry
TRAMMEL Lenard	m	0-10	HOLT Malicey	m	*21-45
WAGNOR A J	m	18-21	HOLT Marthey	f	16+
CANNON William	m	18-21	HOLT Amanda	f	0-16
CANNON Marthey	f	0-16	HOLT Hanna	m*	10-18
GRIGG F W	m	18-21	HOLT Alfred	m	18-21
GRIGG Mary J	f	0-16			
GRIGG Robt	m	10-18	[342]		
GRIGG Albert	m	0-10	PHILIPPS John	m	18-21
GRIGG Ora	f	0-16	PHILIPPS Tho	m	0-10
GRIGG Mary	f	0-16	PHILLPPS Julia	f	0-16
HENSON J N	m	18-21	PHILLIPPS John	m	0-10
MARRS James	m	45+	MALONE Moses	m	21-45
MARRS Mary A	No	entry	MALONE Wm J	m	18-21
WATERS Amanda	f	0-16	MALONE Mary J	f	0-16
BANKS Jordon	m	21-45	MALONE Sarah E	m*	45+
BANKS Sunsan A	f	0-16	MALONE J L	m	10-18
BANKS M A	f	0-16	MALONE Margret	f	0-16
BANKS T A	f	0-16	TOWSWELL Tho	m	10-18
BANKS L M	f	0-16	HAIL Jas	m	18-21
BANKS A H	m	18-21	HAIL N J	m	18-21
BANKS Jas M	m	10-18	YOUNG N M	m	45+
BANKS S E	m	45+	YOUNG Catherine	No	entry
BANKS A J	m	45+	ROSS V A	f	0-16
			ROSS Henreata	f	16+
[340]			ROSS W A	m	18-21
BANKS J W	m	18-21	ROSS Sarah A	f	0-16
ROBBERTS Mary	No	entry	ROSS John T	m	18-21
GREATHOUSE Robt	m	45+	ROSS L M	m	10-18
GREATHOUSE Margret	f	16+	ROSS Mary E	f	0-16
GREATHOUSE B C	m	18-21	ROSS Fanney	f	0-16
GREATHOUSE A T	m	10-18	ROSS Medlin	f	0-16
GREATHOUSE D W	m	10-18	ROSS Charles	m	0-10
GREATHOUSE Sarah	f	16+	RIEFF John	No	entry
GREATHOUSE Dora	f	16+	LOOPER Jas	m	10-18

LOOPER Mary	f	0-16	BOYD John	m	0-10
LOOPER Tho	m	10-18	BOYD James	m	0-10
TAYLOR Steward	m	45+	BOYD Nancy	f	0-16
TAYLOR Elizabeath	No entry		MACKEY R W	m	18-21
			OXFORD Jacob	m	45+
[345]			OXFORD Rebeca	f	16+
BANKS Jordon E	m	10-18	OXFORD Joshiway	m	10-18
BANKS Tho S	m	0-10	OXFORD Eliz	f	0-16
GLAISBROOKS Richard	m	18-21	OXFORD Narsis	f	0-16
GLAISBROOKS Nancy	f	0-16	CORNEALSON Elizabeath	f	16+
GLAISBROOKS Eliza	f	0-16	TOLLET W J	m	21-45
BANKS Thomas	m	21-45	TOLLET Marthey	f	16+
BANKS Rebeca	f	0-16	TOLLET Henry	m	10-18
BANKS Melviney	f	0-16	TOLLET Temperance	f	0-16
BANKS Ellen B	No entry		TOLLET Tho	m	10-18
BANKS George M	m	18-21	TOLLET Elizabeath	f	0-16
BANKS J L	m	21-45	TOLLET William	m	0-10
BANKS Marthey	m	0-16			
BANKS Doug	m	0-10	[349]		
BANKS Simmey	m	45+	TOLLET R C	No entry	
BANKS Ellen	m*	45+	TOLLET Marthey	f	16+
TOLLET Henry	m	21-45	TOLLET Albert	m	10-18
TOLLET Eliza	f	0-16	TOLLET Carrol	m	0-10
TOLLET F G	m	21-45	TOLLET Henry	m	0-10
TOLLET Edward	m	0-10	TOLLET Emma	f	16+
STEAVENS Abiel	m	21-45	MORTON James	m	21-45
STEAVENS Nancy	f	0-16	MORTON Harriet	f	16+
STEAVENS Marthey	f	0-16	MORTON William C	m	0-16
STEAVENS L E	m	45+	BARRINGTON Margret	f	16+
PINKMAN Samuel	m	21-45	BARRINGTON James	m	18-21
STRIPLAN Sarah	f	0-16	BARRINGTON Mary	No entry	
HUET Angeline	f	0-16	[Line left blank by enumerator]		
HUET Ammanda	f	0-16	BOID Wm	m	45+
HUET Rebeca	m*	45+	BOYED Elizabeth	f	16+
HUET Cate	m*	45+	BOYED William	m	10-18
HUET Charls	m	10-18	BOYED Benjman F	m	10-18
			BOYED Clemantyne	f	0-16
[347]			JOHNSON Levina	f	16+
HUET Jeffison	m	0-10	JOHNSON Martha	f	0-16
HUET Emley	f	0-16	JOHNSON Cristian	f	0-16
HUET Robt	m	0-10	JOHNSON Sereona	f	0-16
HUET Ellen	f	0-16	JOHNSON Maggret	f	0-16
BOYD Willice	m	45+	DAVIS Wm	m	0-10
BOYD Leucinda	f	16+	WALKER Cilrany	m	21-45
BOD John T	m	18-21	WALKER Maryea	f	16+
BOYD A M	m	10-18	WALKER Mary	f	0-16
BOYD Darcada	f	0-16	WALKER Fonda	m	0-10
BOYD Darcus	f	16+	WALKER Susan	No entry	
BOYD C M	m	10-18	WALKER Henrey	m	10-18
BOYD W N	m	10-18	DAVIS Susan	m*	45+
BOYD Leucinda	f	0-16			

[351]

BOYD F M	m	21-45
BOYD Arminty	f	0-16
HAMBLEN Eliza	f	45
HAMBLEN James	m	18-21
HAMBLEN Addren	m	10-18
HAMBLEN Andrew	m	10-18
HAMBLEN Mattie	f	0-16
HAMBLEN Jorge	m	0-10
HAMBLEN John	m	0-10
HAMBLEN Marey	f	0-16
WILLIAMS J C	m	21-45
WILLIAMS Martha	f	16+
WILLIAMS Mantta	f	0-16
WILLIAMS Susan F	f	0-16
FERGUSON Joel	m	21-45
FERGUSON Emley	f	0-16
FERGUSON John S	m	0-10
FERGUSON Joel H	m	0-10
FERGUSON James M	m	0-10
FINCHER James A	m	21-45
FINCHER Susan	f	0-16
FINCHER Wm H	m	0-10
HOWLL Sarah	f	16+
HOWLL Marey	f	0-16
HOWLL John W	m	18-21
HOWLL Lafayette	m	10-18
HOWELL Preston	m	0-10
HOWELL _____	m	0-10
HOWELL Sarah E	f	0-16
HOWELL Thomas	m	10-18

[353]

HOWEL Margret	f	16+
HOWEL William	m	0-10
HUET Matilda	f	16+
HUET John W	m	10-18
HUET Robt J	m	0-10
BATES James	m	18-21
BATES Nancy	f	16+
BATES Susan	f	0-16
BATES Henrey	m	0-10
BATES John	m	0-10
BATES James	m	0-10
GODDARD T M	m	18-21
GODDARD Lucinda J	f	16+
GODDARD Marey	f	0-16
GODDARD Charillo J	f	0-16
ANDERSON Samuel	m	21-45
ANDERSON Sarah	f	0-16
ANDERSON Wm	m	10-18

ANDERSON James	m	10-18
ANDERSON Samuel	m	10-18
ANDERSON Eliza J	f	0-16
ANDERSON Nancy A	f	0-16
ANDERSON Matilda	f	0-16
ANDERSON Levina	f	0-16
PENSAN Marey	f	16+
GODDRAD Green	m	18-21
GODDRADE Jane	f	0-16
GODDRAD Samuell	m	0-10
GODDRAD Marey	f	0-16
GODDRED Luretty	f	0-16

[356]

HOLCOMB John	m	45+
HOLCOMB Daley	f	16+
HOLCOMB S M	m	10-18
SMILEY B T	m	10-18
SMILEY John H	m	10-18
HOLCOMB Gorge W	m	10-18
BINAM H D	m	21-45
STELLE Sarad	m	45+
STELLE Sarah E	f	16+
STELLE John T	m	10-18
STELLE A P	m	0-10
TROTT J J	m	45+
TROTT Jame	f	16+
TROTT A H	m	18-21
TROTT James	m	18-21
TROTT Wm	m	0-10
TROTT Charls	m	0-10
TROTT M J	f	0-16
TROTT Polley A	f	0-16
BARNETT James	m	45+
BARNETT Sarann	f	16+
BARNETT James M	m	10-18
BARNETT Leucinda	f	16+
BARNETT Milisa J	f	0-16
BARNETT Nancy	f	0-16
BARNETT Sarah C	f	0-16
THOMAS John	m	21-45
THOMAS Mrs.	f	16+
THOMAS (4 Children)	m	10-18

[358]

CHESHER John B	m	45+
CHESHER Juda	f	16+
CHESHER Marey	f	16+
CHESHER Martha	f	16+
CHESHER Wm	m	10-18
CHESHER Elizabeth	f	0-16

CHESHER John	m	0-10	BURKS Elizabeath	f	16+
CHESHER Laney	f	0-16	BURKS Vallenhan	f	0-16
CHESHER Ella	f	0-16			
STANFIELD Lavina	f	16+	[362]		
STANFIELD Wm	m	18-21	ARNOLD G W	m	21-45
STANFIELD Edward	m	10-18	ARNOLD Julian	m	0-10
FREYSCHLAG E	f	0-16	ARNOLD Clearsey	f	0-16
FREYSCHLAG Lucia	f	16+	ARNOLD A C	f	0-16
FREYSCHLAG Safa	f	16+	ARNOLD Emiline	f	0-16
FREYSCHLAG Gorge	m	10-18	EDDONS Emeline	f	0-16
FREYSCHLAG Jane	f	0-16	GREGG M S	m	45+
FREYSCHLAG Marey	f	0-16	GREGG S	f	16+
FREYSCHLAG James	m	0-10	GREGG B W	m	21-45
ANDERSON Robet	m	21-45	GREGG Jane	f	16+
ANDERSON Cornealin	f	16+	GREGG Henry	m	10-18
SHELTON Polley	f	16+	GREGG Sefronie	f	0-16
SKELTON Luiza	f	16+	GREGG Lafayet	m	0-10
SKELTON Matha	f	16+	GREGG Hellen	m*	0-10
SKELTON Ameida	f	16+	JOHNSON Wm	m	21-45
SKELTON Orlesia	f	0-16	JOHNSON Sarah	f	16+
DENEY Marey	f	16+	JOHNSON Marthey	f	0-16
			JOHNSON John	m	10-18
[360]			JOHNSON Tho	m	0-10
WOOD Andrew	m	21-45	JOHNSON Elizabeath	f	0-16
WOOD Flora	f	16+	KINNEBROUG John	m	21-45
WOOD Marey F	f	0-16	KENNEBROUG Rebeca J	f	16+
WOOD J W	m	0-10	KINNEBROUG C H	m	18-21
WOOD James A	m	0-10	KIMBROUGH Mary	f	0-16
WOOD Nesan	m	21-45	KINNEBROUG James	m	10-18
WOOD Sarah	f	16+	KINNBRGH Marthey	f	0-16
WOOD Anthan	m	0-10	KENNIABROUGH Isabla	f	0-16
WOOD John	m	0-10	KINNIBRGH Harriet	f	0-16
WOOD Gorge	m	0-10	KINNEBROUGH R E	f	0-16
WOOD Edward	m	0-10			
FURGERSON Jas	m	21-45	[364]		
FURGERSON Harriet L	f	16+	McCOLLUM Robt	m	21-45
LADD W H	m	21-45	McCOLLUM Sefronie	f	16+
LADD Julia E	f	16+	McCOLLUM Ransom	m	10-18
PITTMAN S M	m	21-45	THOMAS Margret	f	16+
PITTMAN Sallia	No entry		HOWEL Clark	m	21-45
PITTMAN Willie	m	0-10	HOWEL Mary	f	16+
PITTMAN Mary D	f	16+	HOWEL Mary F	f	0-16
PITTMAN J M	m	21-45	HOWEL Josefus	m	0-10
PITTMAN W E	m	21-45	BOON Levy	m	45+
REED G W M	No entry		BOON Mark W	m	18-21
SEYMOUR Robt	m	45+	BOON William B	m	10-18
SEYMOUR Charls	m	10-18	BOON J W	m	10-18
SEYMOUR R E	m	10-18	POOL A C	m	21-45
SEYMOUR Marier	f	16+	POOL Mary J	m*	10-18
SEYMOUR Hellen	f	16+	POOL George W	m	10-18
BURKS Kesey	m	21-45	POOL Leucinda E	f	0-16

POOL Emley C	f	0-16	LILES Nancy E		f	16+
POOL Margret S	f	0-16	LILES Josephet		m	18-21
REED A W	m	21-45	LILES Henry R		m	18-21
REED Elizabeath	f	16+	LILES Wm C		m	10-18
REED Mary E	f	0-16	LILES Mary E		f	0-16
REED Robt H	m	0-10	LILES Emley F		f	0-16
REED John A	m	0-10	DUNLAP Francis		f	16+
BARRENS Wiley	m	21-45	DYE William S		m	21-45
BARRENS Amanda	f	16+	DYE Susan F		f	16+
BARRES E M	f	0-16	DYE Mary		f	0-16
PYATT E	f	16+	NEAL Alexander		m	45+
PYATT J C	m	21-45	NEAL Martha		f	16+
PYATT W H	m	21-45	NEAL Sarah Jane		f	16+
PYATT J P	m	21-45	NEAL Mary		f	16+
			NEAL E M		f	16+
[366]			NEAL William J		m	45+
MAXWELL J J	m	21-45	NEAL John C		m	45+
MAXWEL Manervey	f	16+	NEAL Andrew		m	10-18
MAXWELL Eliz	f	16+	NEAL Alexander B		m	10-18
MAXWELL Robt	m	10-18	NEAL H H		m	0-10
MAXWELL Wm	m	10-18	ALEXANDER Mary		f	16+
MAXWELL Jas	m	0-10	ALEXANDER Mary A		f	0-16
BARKER Tho	m	21-45	REED Samual		m	45+
BARKER Lousa	f	16+	REED Salley		f	16+
BARKER Wm	m	0-10	REED Haner Jane		f	0-16
BARKER John	m	0-10	REED G Sumter		m	0-10
EASON Wm	m	45+	REED Mary		f	0-16
EASON Susan	f	16+				
EASON Henry	m	18-21	[370]			
EASON Mary	f	0-16	REED Martha		f	0-16
EASON Sam	m	10-18	INGRAM Albert		m	0-10
SMITH William	m	10-18	WILSON John		m	45+
SMITH Eliz	f	0-16	WILSON Elizabeath		f	16+
SMITH Ellen	f	0-16	WILSON J M C		m	21-45
SMITH George	No entry		WILSON William C		m	18-21
SMITH Alenia	f	0-16	BRONANBURG Leucindia		f	16+
WEBB Benjamon	m	45+	BRONANBURG G W		m	21-45
WEBB Nancy	f	0-16	BRONANBURG S F		m	21-45
WEBB Jane	f	16+	REED Gorge W C		m	21-45
WEBB George Alison	m	0-10	REED Margret		f	16+
WILSON John R	f*	0-16	REED Sarah Jane		f	0-16
WILSON Malvina	f	16+	REED Catharine		f	0-16
WILSON Flory	f	16+	REED Luisa		f	0-16
WILSON Fany	f	16+	REED Mary		f	0-16
WILSON Mary	f	16+	REED Easter		f	0-16
WILSON Edord	m	0-10	REED Jones		m	0-10
			REED James		m	0-10
[368]			REED Matildia		f	0-16
WILSON F	f	0-16	HOPE Ralph J		m	45+
WILSON Frankling	m	0-10	HOPE Lucindia J		f	0-16
LILES E S	f	0-16	RAMY L H		m	10-18

1865 SHERIFF'S CENSUS OF WASHINGTON COUNTY ARKANSAS

Name	Sex	Age	Name	Sex	Age
RAMY Sarah	m*	45+	TAYLER Enich Lafayett	m	0-10
CROFFORD John	m	45+	TAYLER T J	m	18-21
CROFFORD W	f	0-16	TAYLER John Scot	m	0-10
CROFFRD Malindia C	m*	45+	MASHBURN M A	f	16+
CROFFORD Any E	m*	45+	REED E	m	18-21
CROFFORD William J	m	0-10	MASHBURN J H	m	18-21
CROFFORD Sarah E	m*	45+	MASHBURN J M	m	18-21
			MASHBURN J H		No entry
[372]			MASHBURN S	m	0-10
HOMSLEY Levi	m	45+	THURMAN John	m	45+
HOMSLEY Alice	f	0-16	THURMAN Jane	f	16+
HOMSLEY B W	m	21-45	THURMAN William	m	21-45
HOMSLEY W S	m	18-21	THURMAN M E	f	0-16
HOMSLEY Mary L	m*	45+	THURMAN N N	m	18-21
HOMSLEY G A	m	10-18	THURMAN John S	m	21-45
HOMSLEY J G	m	10-18	THURMAN Salla	f	0-16
HOMSLEY Levi T	m	0-10	THURMAN _	f	0-16
HOMSLEY S P	f	0-16	THURMAN __lias	f	0-16
ROBERTS Any	f	16+			
ROBERTS W J	m	21-45	[376]		
ROBTS Catharine	f	0-16	THURMAN Elisea	f	0-16
ROBTS Adeline	f	0-16	RIEFF O M	m	45+
ROBTS Sena	f	0-16	RIEFF M A	f	16+
ROBTS Osco	f	0-16	RIEFF M J	f	0-16
Andrew	m	0-10	RIEFF E C	f	0-16
WELLS W A	m	21-45	RIEFF M D	f	0-16
WELLS Salla	f	16+	RIEFF H M	m	21-45
PAYTON Luis	m	0-10	RIEFF Lura	f	16+
SMITH A C	m	45+	RIEFF O M Jn	m	10-18
SMITH A J	m	21-45	RIEFF John _	m	45+
SMITH T	f	0-16	RIEFF Catharine	f	16+
McROY H A	m	10-18	RIEFF James F	m	0-10
KEEN Mary P	f	16+	DEATHEROW Joel	m	45+
GIBSON Gorge	m	45+	DEATHEROW M	f	16+
GIBSON Margret	f	0-16	DEATHEROW M E	f	16+
GIBSON Sarah	f	0-16	DEATHEROW Sarah An	f	16+
KEEN William	m	0-10	DEATHEROW Haley	f	16+
KEEN __rge	m	0-10	DEATHEROW Mary	f	0-16
			DEATHEROW E	f	16+
[374]			CRISPS Gorge	m	18-21
RICE A	m	21-45	CRISPS John	m	10-18
RICE Mary Adline	f	0-16	Caldona	f	0-16
RICE Scinthey A	m*	45+	WILSON James F	m	45+
RICE Mary E	f	0-16	WILSON Rose	f	16+
RICE John	m	0-10	CABE J C	f*	0-16
TAYLER Alford	m	45+	CABE Margret	f	16+
TAYLER Maryan	f	16+	E CABE	m	10-18
TAYLER Sarah E	f	0-16			
TAYLER Isabel Jane	f	0-16	[378]		
TAYLER A J	m	18-21	MATHAS Wilborn	m	45+
TAYLER H M	f	0-16	MATHEWES Chriestene	f	16+

56

1865 SHERIFF'S CENSUS OF WASHINGTON COUNTY ARKANSAS

MATHEWES Peter	m	45+	CAMBES Sarah	f	0-16
MATHEWES Callonda	f	0-16	YOES Enos W	m	18-21
MATHEWES John	m	10-18	YOES Abbegale	f	0-16
MATHEWES Jackson	m	10-18	YOES James W	m	10-18
MATHEWS Lycergus	No entry		YOES Sarah	f	0-16
MATHEWES Sarah	No entry				
MATHEWES Frankling	No entry		[382]		
MATHEWS Elen	f	0-16	HOLCOMB W G	m	21-45
KELLEY C E	m	45+	HOLCOMB F E	f	0-16
KELLEY Sarah G	f	16+	HOLCOMB J R	m	10-18
KELLEY Wm Arter	m	10-18	HOLCOMB M E	f	16+
KELLEY Francis M	m	0-10	HOLCOMB Martha	f	0-16
KELLEY Tennesee Jane	f	0-16	HOLCOMB S E	f	0-16
KELLEY R C	m	0-10	WOODRUFF J N	m	21-45
KELLEY Jasper N	m	0-16	WOODRUFF Martha	m*	45+
JOHNSON P	m	45+	WOODRUFF L	f	0-16
JOHNSON Catharine	f	16+	WOODRUFF J	m	0-10
JOHNSON M J	f	0-16	WOODRUFF V	f	16+
JOHNSON Sarah C	f	0-16	WOODRUFF J	m	10-18
JOHNSON Luisa C	f	0-16	HOLCOMB G W	f	0-16
JOHNSON M E	f	0-16	HOLCOMB N	f	0-16
JOHNSON William	No entry		WOODRUFF F M	m	21-45
DUNLAP Joseph	m	45+	WOODRUFF Jemima	No entry	
DUNLAP Mary Jane	f	16+	WOODRUFF Comell	m	45+
DUNLAP Wm F	m	0-10	WOODRUFF E	m	10-18
DUNLAP G W	m	0-10	WOODRUFF Maud	f	0-16
DUNLAP J Henry	m	0-10	WOODRUFF Sarah	f	16+
DUNLAP _ule E	f	0-16	WOODRUFF John	f*	16+
			NORWOD Magat	f	16+
			NORWOD Susan	f	0-16
[380]			NORWOD Austan	m	10-18
DUNLOP Benjaman	m	0-10	NORWOD Thomas	m	10-18
MARTIN William	m	21-45	PALSTON Jane	f	0-16
MARTIN Lucindia	f	16+			
MARTIN Analisa	f	0-16			
MARTIN Mary Jane	f	0-16	[384]		
MARTIN Rodoafels Adline	f	0-16			
William	No entry		PALSTON Martha	f	0-16
Alexander		45+	PATTAN C	m	0-10
ALEXANDER Mary E	f	0-16	JANES Elisha	m	21-45
ALEXANDER John C	m	18-21	JANES Margat	No entry	
ALEXANDER Samuel H	m	18-21	JANES John T	m	18-21
ALLEXANDER Tempey	m	45+	JANES James T	m	10-18
BLOYD Eli	m	45+	JANES Mary M	m*	45+
CAMBES Joel A	m	45+	WILLSON Thomas	m	21-45
CAMBES Ornetta	f	16+	WILLSON Sharlat	m*	45+
CAMBES Mary M	f	0-16	WILLSON Armenta	f	0-16
CAMBES Francis E	f	0-16	WILLSON Julian	f	0-16
CAMBES Cefronia	f	0-16	WILLSON Rachal M	f	16+
CAMBES Caldonia	f	16+	WILLSON V	f	0-16
CAMBES Miles M	m	18-21	QUILLEN John	No entry	
YOES Jacob	m	18-21	QUILLEN Caroline	f	0-16

QUELEN Elizabeth	f	0-16
QULLEN Joseph	m	10-18
QUELEN William	m	10-18
QUELLEN Margat	No entry	
QULLEN James	m	10-18
QUELLEN Martha	f	16+
PEARCE John	m	10-18
HUTCHENS John	m	21-45
HUTCHENS Jane	f	0-16
HUTCHENS Thomas	m	10-18
GILLENSWATER Mary	m*	45+
GILLENSWATER E	m	18-21
GILLENSWATER T G	m	10-18
GILLENSWATER M E	f	16+

[386]
TAYLOR A	m	21-45
TAYLOR S A	m	45+
EDMERSON Nancy J	f	16+
EDMERSON Amandia	f	0-16
EDMERSAN F	f	0-16
EDMESSON J W	m	10-18
TAYLOR T A	m	10-18
PHILLIPS L	m	21-45
PHILLIPES Susan H	f	0-16
PHILLIPES James C	m	10-18
PHILLIPES Allen A	m	18-21
PHILLIPES N A	m	10-18
PHILLIPES M A	f	0-16
PHILLIPES A E	f	16+
ROBETES Mary	f	0-16
PEARSON Ester	f	0-16
PEARSON John	m	10-18
PEARSON Sarah	f	16+
PEARSON Elizabet	f	0-16
PEARSON Robert	m	10-18
PEARSON Luvenia	f	16+
PEARSON Jane	f	0-16
PEARSON Anna	f	0-16
CATO Jacob	m	21-45
CATO Luntisha	f	0-16
CATO John	m	18-21
CATO Joseph	m	10-18
CATO James	m	10-18

[388]
PRAIRIE TOWNSHIP
BURRIS J W	m	10-18
BURRIS A M	f	16+
BURRIS Lockey	f	0-16
BURRIS Matilda D	f	0-16

WILSON L H	m	21-45
WILSON Rachal	f	16+
WILSON Henry	m	10-18
WILSON Bracken	m	10-18
WILSON Mary E	f	0-16
WILSON Tho	m	10-18
WILSON Sarah	m*	0-10
WILSON Sarah	m*	10-18
WILSON Charls	m	10-18
WILSON Lidda	f	0-16
WILSON Wm	No entry	
WILSON Zackrier	m	0-10
WOODRUFF Wrett	m	18-21
WOODRUFF S S	m	10-18
WOODRUFF Wm	m	0-10
WOODRUFF Eliza	m*	0-10
WOODRUFF Bill	f*	16+
WOODRUFF Henry	m	0-10
HOLT John	m	18-21
HOLT Emley	f	16+
ROGERS Dinarza	f	16+
ROGERS Wm T	m	0-10
ROGERS Nancy J	f	0-16
ROGERS Hanna	f	0-16
ROGERS John D	m	0-10
MICHEL Wm	m	18-21
MICHEL Josfin	m*	18-21

[390]
LEWIS Va	No entry	
LEWIS W M	No entry	
MALONE John P	m	0-10
MALONE M M	m	0-10
MALONE J M	m	0-10
RUTHERFORD Cansedey	f	16+
RUTHERFORD Malinda E	f	0-16
RUTHERFORD Wm M	m	21-45
MATHEWES J M	No entry	
LEWIS A B	m	18-21
WOLSEY Matilda	f	16+
WOLSEY Leuraney	f	16+
WOLSEY Louiza	f	16+
STEAVERSON Nancy	f	16+
COLENDER Jane	f	16+
COLENDER Alfred	m	18-21
COLENDER J E	m	18-21
COLENDER Wm	m	10-18
COLENDER Jas	m	0-10
COLENDER Nancy E	f	0-16
COLENDER Isaac	m	0-10
COLENDER Zale H	m	0-10

COLENDER Tennisee	f	0-16	BLAKEY Leannora	f	0-16
CRAVEN Sarh	f	16+	ROCKSON J T	m	18-21
CRAVEN Elizabeath	f	0-16	WATES J H	m	18-21
CRAVEN John	m	0-10	WATES S J	f	16+
CRAVEN Liza J	f	0-16	WATES W W	m	0-10
CRAVEN Tassey	f	0-16	WATES Nathan	m	0-10
TILMAN N J	m	18-21	WATES J M	m	0-10
TILMAN Mary M	f	16+	WILLIAMS W H	m	18-21
TILMAN J___ N	m	0-10	WILSON Jas C	m	18-21
			WILSON J M	f	16+
[393]			WILSON M M	f	16+
CITY OF FAYETTEVILLE			WILSON W D	m	10-18
WATSON C L	f	16+	PARKS Margret	m*	FPC
WATSON Clem	f	16+	CUNNINGHAM Nicklous	f*	FPC
WATSON Joseph	m	18-21	VANWRINKLE Squire	m	FPC
WATSON Charles R	m	10-18			
WATSON E P	m	10-18	[397]		
JOBE D B	m	21-45	VAUGHN Eliza	f	FPC
JOBE E L	f	16+	HOLT E F	m	21-45
JOBE Leanora	f	0-16	HOLT J D	f	0-16
JOBE D L R	m	0-10	HOLT C D	m	10-18
STONE S K	No entry		HOLT E F	m	0-10
STONE A M	f	16+	HOLT M F	m	0-10
STONE Robt	m	18-21	REED G W M	m	21-45
STONE B H	m	10-18	REED Mary J	f	16+
STONE Wm C	m	10-18	REED Elizabeath M	f	0-16
STONE Lodwick	m	0-10	REED Margret M	f	0-16
STONE Amanda	f	16+	REED John A	m	0-10
STONE Albert	m	0-10	REED Angaline	f	0-16
ALBRIGHT George S	m	21-45	REED G W M	m	0-10
ALBRIGHT Mary M	f	16+	REED Marthey	f	16+
ALBRIGHT S K	m	0-10	REED Susan E	f	16+
HARDEN W E	m	21-45	STARK D D	No entry	
HARDEN Harry P	m	10-18	LACK C A	m	21-45
HARDEN Henderson	m	10-18	LACK J E	f	16+
HARDEN Marthey	f	16+	CARTER Thomas	m	21-45
HARDEN Anderson	m	0-10	CARTER Margret J	f	16+
HARDEN Margret	f	16+	CARTER William E	m	0-10
			CARTER Mary	f	0-16
[395]			CARTER Allice B	f	0-16
JACK Abrem	m	21-45	WING Senacy	m	18-21
JACK Elizabeath	f	16+	WING S H	f	16+
JACK Henry	m	18-21	KING Lee O	m	18-21
JACK Wlliam	m	10-18	KING _____	f	0-16
SUTTON Henry	m	18-21			
CARLILE Tho J	m	18-21	[399]		
CARLILE M A	f	16+	BAUM Moses	m	18-21
CARLILE Allice P	f	0-16	ADKINS John	m	FPC
CARLILE Margret	f	0-16	ADKINS Jane	f	FPC
BLAKELEY John L	m	18-21	ADKINS David	m	FPC
BLAKLEY E J	f	16+	ADKINS John	m	FPC

1865 SHERIFF'S CENSUS OF WASHINGTON COUNTY ARKANSAS

SUTTON Jas	m	21-45		BUI John	m	21-45
SUTTON Fracean	f	16+		BUI _ _	f	16+
SUTTON Wm S	m	0-10				
SUTTON Mary B	f	0-16		[403]		
SUTTON Isabella	f	16+		BUI H F	m	10-18
SUTTON George	m	10-18		BUI Mary J	f	0-16
COFFEY W A	m	18-21		BUI Sarah C	f	0-16
COFFEY C B	m	10-18		BOWERS Leurcrise	No	entry
COFFEY Margret	f	16+		BOWERS Christopher	m	0-10
COFFEY D W	m	10-18		JERRIGAN L D	m	18-21
COFFEY G M	m	0-10		BATEPHUR H C C	m	18-21
RIEFF Henry	m	18-21		BATEFIPER Milley	f	16+
RIEFF Sarah fO	f	16+		BATEFPR Mltes	f	0-16
RIEFF Henry M	m	18-21		MITCHEL R	m	18-21
RIEFF John E H	f*	0-16		MITCHEL Angeline	f	0-16
RIEFF Lizzie H	f	0-16		MITCHEL J S	m	0-10
KISER Henry	m	21-45		MITCHEL Mary J	f	0-16
KISER Nancy A	f	16+		ZILLEH Joseph	m	21-45
KISER Henry Jr	f*	16+		ZILLEH C	f	16+
KISER William	m	0-10		ZILLEH John	m	0-10
AIKEN W G	m	21-45		CARLILE Jas	m	21-45
AIKEN S S	f	16+		CARLILE Annaliza	f	16+
AIKENS _____	m	0-10		CARLILE J H	m	0-10
				CARLILE N B	m	0-10
[401]				CARLILE S J	m	0-10
JACKSON C	m	18-21		CARLILE W H	m	0-10
JACKSON Sarah	f	16+		CARLILE J M	m	0-10
JACKSON Evrate	f	0-16		TAYLOR Isaac	m	18-21
JACKSON Wayman	m	0-10		TAYLOR Margret J	f	16+
JACKSON U S	m	0-10		TAYLOR Jas L	m	0-10
JACKSON Allice	f	0-16		TAYLOR Williams G	m	0-10
GREGG Lafayete	m	18-21				
GREGG Mary A	f	16+		[405]		
GREGG A W	m	0-10		BONNUM M G	m	21-45
GREGG A S	m	0-10		BONNUM Margret L	f	16+
GREGG Willey	m	0-10		BONNUM Alzene J	f	0-16
DEABENPORT C H	m	18-21		BONNUM Tho E	m	0-10
DEABENPORT M J	f	16+		DYE Thomas	m	45+
DEABENPORT D W C	m	0-10		HODGES Alic	f	16+
BENROOK John	m	18-21		HODGES Robt	m	18-21
BENBROOK Mary J	f	16+		HODGES Sarah	f	16+
BENBROOK Allice C	f	0-16		HODGES Magnolia	f	0-16
BENBROOKS Albert L	m	0-10		HODGES James	m	0-10
BENBROOK Manervey C	f	0-16		BARNES Elizabeath	f	16+
JACK William A	m	45+		BARNES Mary V	f	16+
JACK E	f	16+		BARROUS Angeline	f	0-16
JACK Thomas	m	0-10		BARROUS James	f*	0-16
JACK Martha	f	0-16		CROUCH Adison	m	21-45
JACK T___	m	0-10		CROUCH Jane	f	16+
JACK Jacob	m	0-10		CROUCH Henry L	m	10-18
JACK Nancy	f	0-16		CROUCH C M	m	18-21

CROUCH Walter	m	10-18
CROUCH Edward	m	0-10
CROUCH William	m	0-10
CROUCH L C	m	0-10
CROUCH Mguire	f	0-16
CROUCH Dora	f	0-16
BASSORE Demaice	f	16+
PLEASANCE Demacie	f	16+

ROBBINSON 9 15 42
ROBBISON 15
ROBBISTS 20
ROBBNSON 9 42
ROBERSON 15
ROBERTS 56
ROBERTSON 15
ROBETES 58
ROBINSON 15 42
ROBTS 56
ROCKSON 59
ROGERS 15 58
ROGGERS 24
ROHL 16
ROIRTS 16
ROMERY 20
ROSE 10 11
ROSS 17 23 51
RUNNELS 41 50
RUSSEL 22
RUTHERFORD 24 31-35 39
    40 58
SANDERS 7 30 48
SAWYERS 29 30 33 34
SCHOOTE 28
SCOTT 25
SEAGER 13
SEARCEY 3
SEARCY 3
SEAVERS 13
SEAY 13 20 21
SECENBOY 38
SENCYBOY 38
SEXTON 21
SEYMOUR 54
SHANNON 13 18 33 34
SHARP 1 23 28 31 33
    50
SHEALDS 50
SHELTON 54
SHEPARD 9
SHERA 12
SHERROD 2 45
SHIPLEY 19
SHORES 11
SHRA 12
SHUMATE 48 49
SIMES 2
SIMPSON 18 19 21 28
    32
SINKLER 36
SIZEMOORE 11
SIZMOORE 11

SKELTON 54
SMEDLEY 35
SMILEY 2 4 8 53
SMITH 1 4 6 12 13 18
    19 32 45 46 50
    55 56
SNEAD 3
SONS 9
SPENCER 23
SPRIGSTON 44
STAFFORD 2 4
STAFORD 2
STANFIELD 54
STANLEY 5
STARK 59
STEAVENS 25 52
STEAVERSON 58
STEEL 6
STELLE 53
STEVEN 48
STEVENS 48
STEVERSON 16
STEWARD 19 44
STEWARDST 26
STEWART 26
STINNET 44
STINNETT 44
STOCKBUGAR 35 36
STOKENBERRY 47
STONE 4 59
STOUT 41 42
STRAIN 43 49
STRICKLEN 36
STRICKLER 27 28 30 39
    40
STRIPLAN 52
STWED 44
SUMATE 49
SUNATE 49
SUTTON 59 60
TALLS 9
TANKERSLEY 31 32 34
TAWLER 49
TAYLER 56
TAYLOR 37 52 58 60
TENNANT 18
TERRY 6
THARP 41
THOMAS 53 54
THOMASON 15
THOMISON 14
THOMPSON 41 44 49
THOMSON 16 17

THORNSBERRY 6
THURMAN 56
TILMAN 59
TIMBS 12
TINNEN 33
TINS 20
TOHOMSON 16
TOLLET 52
TOWSWELL 51
TRAMMEL 50 51
TRENT 12
TROTT 53
TRUET 29
TUNE 38, 39
TUNN 38
UUSE 41
VANCE 30 31
VANHOOSE 42 43
VANWRINKLE 59
VAUGHN 47 48 59
VERNON 3 5
VINZANT 45
WADKINS 50
WAGNON 16
WAGNOR 51
WAITS 50
WALKER 7 8 13 52
WALKUP 48
WALLER 13
WALUP 48
WARD 48
WARSON 5
WASHBURN 12
WASHINGTON 18
WATERS 5 6 19 51
WATES 59
WATSON 59
WEATHERSHOON 25
WEAVER 24
WEBB 55
WEBBER 26 32
WEBSTER 5 7
WEEB 38 46
WEESE 25
WELCH 24
WELDON 11
WELLS 56
WEST 9 10 13-15 25
    32 33 39 43 50
WHEALER 32
WHITE 2-4 23 28 31
    49
WHITSET 33

WILCOX 16 20
WILHITE 28
WILLIAM 48
WILLIAMES 46
WILLIAMS 23 25 27 43
     45-50 53 59
WILLIFORD 46 47 49
WILLIMAS 46
WILLSON 15 57
WILSON 3 9 10 20 55
     56 58 59
WING 59
WINGFIELD 12
WINKLER 42 43
WINN 35 36
WOLSEY 36 58
WOOD 49 54
WOODDY 16
WOODROUGH 20
WOODRUFF 57 58
WOODS 27 35
WRIGHT 26 48
WRITE 19 48
YAGAR 16 21
YAGER 11 21 26
YATES 24
YEAGAR 16
YEAR 16
YOES 57
YONG 39
YOUNG 32 39 51
YUNG 32
ZILLEH 60

www.ingramcontent.com/pod-product-compliance
Lightning Source LLC
Chambersburg PA
CBHW080522090426
42734CB00015B/3137